Contemporary CLASS GUITAP

Book 1

by Will Schr

CONTENTS

This product is available as a BOOK ONLY and as a BOOK/CD package. The CD contains a recorded track for each song in the book. On the CD, the *melody* is on the right side, and the *band only* is on the left side.

HAL•LEONARD® CORPORATION
7777 W. BLUEMOUND RD. P.O. BOX 13819 MILWAUKEE, WI 53213

ABOUT THE AUTHOR

Will Schmid has gained the reputation as an outstanding guitar teacher and performer throughout the United States. He received his BA from Luther College and his PhD from the Eastman School of Music. While teaching at the University of Kansas, he created and performed a series of programs entitled "Folk Music Americana" for National Public Radio. Dr. Schmid is the author of the bestselling **Hal Leonard Guitar Method** (available in 7 languages) and over 30 other books for guitar and banjo. He has given guitar and folk music workshops throughout the United States and Australia. From 1979 to 1981 he was President of the Wisconsin Music Educators Conference. He is currently Associate Professor of Music Education at the University of Wisconsin-Milwaukee and serves on the editorial staff of the Hal Leonard Publishing Corporation.

FOREWORD

The time for **Contemporary Class Guitar** has arrived. Both teachers and students are moving away from one-dimensional guitar instruction toward a holistic (well-rounded) approach to all facets of guitar technique:

- singing and strumming
- note reading and music theory
- finger picking and flat picking
- instrumental solos and guitar ensembles
- improvisation and writing music

Over half of the songs in this book are **contemporary copyrighted songs.** The instruction is sequenced to provide easy access to learning, solid reinforcement of new skills and concepts, and a variety of activities and styles of music. Book 1 of **Contemporary Class Guitar** builds a strong basic technique which can be used as a springboard to such styles as classical, rock, folk, pop, blues, bluegrass and country. Techniques introduced in this book are further developed in Book 2.

This book can be used for either class or individual instruction.

ACKNOWLEDGEMENTS

The author wishes to acknowledge the help provided by thousands of guitar students, ages 10 to 70, on whom these ideas have all been tested, hundreds of school and private guitar teachers who have given valuable feedback and the support of colleagues who believe in the life-long benefits of playing the guitar. A special thanks to the Guitar Shop Ltd. for the loan of the Ramirez guitar on the cover.

HOW TO USE THIS BOOK

The sequence of skills and concepts introduced in this book are based on years of teaching guitar students of all ages in many different contexts. If you learn each new skill carefully and keep reviewing the old skills and familiar songs, your passage through the book should be smooth. Nevertheless, there are individual differences from one student to the next: Some learn faster than others, hands and fingers come in different sizes and some respond differently to singing and playing. For these reasons, both teachers and players should carefully consider the following guidelines:

Sing and Strum: Learning new chords

- Study each new chord diagram carefully. If there are optional ways to play a chord, begin with the easiest and then work on the harder form when you are ready. It is common in a large class to have several forms of the same chord being played simultaneously.
- **Sing and Strum** pages are clearly marked at the edge with a gray stripe. The starting pitch for singing is given in the upper left-hand corner. These pages are intended to help you develop your accompanying skills using the new chords, strums and finger picks introduced throughout the book.
- **Sing and Strum** pages are **not** intended for note reading. The notation is usually more difficult than the reading skills developed on the other pages of the book. This is why the **Sing and Strum** pages are clearly marked.

Playing Notes: Learning to read and play instrumental guitar

- Single-note melodies can be played with a pick or with the thumb or fingers. This book tries to develop a variety of techniques which are appropriate to the styles of guitar which exist today. Give yourself a chance to learn to play several different ways instead of developing only one side of your technique.
- Play each exercise and song carefully and steadily. Repeat each piece until you can play it with ease before going on.
- Keep a steady beat by tapping your foot (toe) or by playing with a metronome.

Learning New Songs

- When learning a new song or instrumental piece, begin at a slower speed, use simple strums until the chords are learned, and then proceed to more difficult techniques.
- On pages not marked as **Sing and Strum** pages, first learn the instrumental melody by reading the notes; then sing if words are given.

Guitar Ensembles: Playing several different parts at the same time

- Throughout the book there are specially marked **Guitar Ensemble** pages which give you the chance to play 2-, 3- and 4-part pieces. If the book is being used by a single player, the tape recorder can be used to simulate a guitar ensemble.
- Most songs and pieces can be played by splitting the class into two or three different roles such as melody (sung and/or played), chords (strummed and/or finger picked) and even a bass line.

Write (Improvise) Your Own Music

- Some suggestions are given throughout the book for helping you to make up your own music. Use these as a beginning and create your own improvisation possibilities with a friend or a tape recorder.

YOUR GUITAR

This book is designed for use with any type of guitar — acoustic steel-string, nylon-string classic or electric. Any of these guitars can be adapted to use in a wide variety of styles of music. Study the names of the guitar parts before progressing to the page on Playing Position.

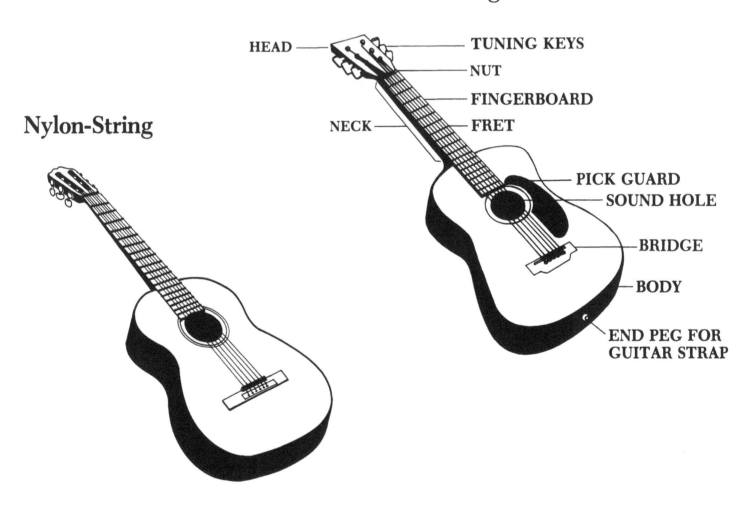

Steel-String

HEAD — TUNING KEYS

NUT

FINGERBOARD

NECK — FRET

PICK GUARD

SOUND HOLE

BRIDGE

BODY

END PEG FOR GUITAR STRAP

Nylon-String

Electric

TOGGLE SWITCH

PICKUPS

VOLUME CONTROLS

TONE CONTROLS

PLAYING POSITION

There are several ways to hold the guitar and sit comfortably while providing a proper playing position. The upper position shown on this page can be used with any type of guitar, but the lower (classical) position is usually used only with nylon-string guitars. Observe the following general guidelines in forming your playing posture:

- Position your body, arms and legs in such a way that you **avoid tension.** If you feel tension creeping into your playing, you probably need to reassess your position.

- Tilt the neck upwards — never down.

- Keep the body of the guitar as vertical as possible. Avoid slanting the top of the guitar so that you can see better.

- Balance your weight evenly from left to right. Sit straight (but not rigid).

TUNING

There are several ways to tune your guitar. You can tune to a piano or organ keyboard, a guitar pitchpipe or one of the new electronic tuners. If no standard pitch source is available, use the section on relative tuning below.

Keyboard

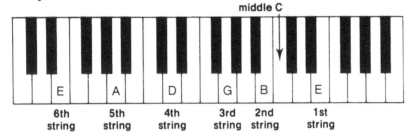

middle C

E	A	D	G	B	E
6th string	5th string	4th string	3rd string	2nd string	1st string

Guitar Pitch Pipe

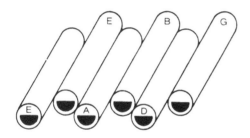

Electronic Guitar Tuner

Relative Tuning

To check or correct your tuning when no pitch source is available, follow these steps:

- Assume that the sixth string is tuned correctly to E.
- Press the sixth string at the 5th fret. This is the pitch A to which you tune your open fifth string. Play the depressed sixth string and the fifth string with your thumb. When the two sounds match, you are in tune.
- Press the fifth string at the 5th fret and tune the open fourth string to it. Follow the same procedure that you did on the fifth and sixth strings.
- Press the fourth string at the 5th fret and tune the open third string to it.
- To tune the second string, press the third string at the 4th fret and tune the open second string to it.
- Press the second string at the 5th fret and tune the first string to it.

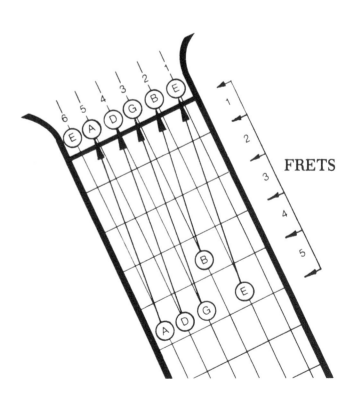

FRETS

LEFT-HAND POSITION

Left-hand fingers are numbered 1 through 4. (Pianists: Note that the thumb is **not** number 1.) Place the thumb in back of the neck roughly opposite the 2nd finger as shown in the illustration below. Avoid gripping the neck like a baseball bat with the palm touching the back of the neck.

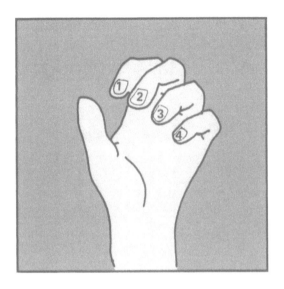 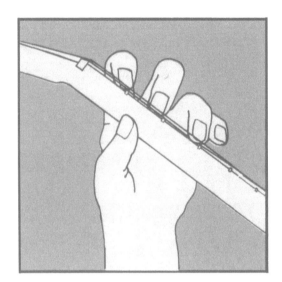

RIGHT-HAND POSITION

The right hand should be positioned in two distinctly different ways depending on whether you are using a pick and strumming (left illustration) or whether you are finger picking (right illustration). The crucial difference can be seen in the wrist height above the strings and in the flatness or roundness of the palm.

 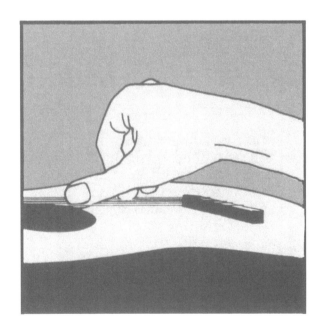

PLAYING CHORDS

A chord is sounded when more than two notes or strings are played at the same time. To begin you will be playing chords on three strings with only one finger depressed. Disregard the light gray finger numbers on strings 4, 5 and 6 until you can easily play the one-finger versions of the chords below.

An (o) under a string indicates that the string should be played "OPEN" (not depressed by a finger).

An (x) under a string indicates that the string should not be strummed.

The C Chord

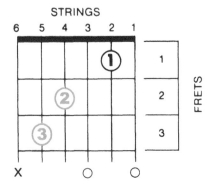

The G7 Chord

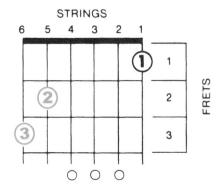

Study the illustration for the one-finger C chord. Do not play fingers 2 and 3 until later when you have mastered the simpler one-finger version. Depress the 2nd string with the tip of your first finger. Arch the finger to avoid touching the 1st string. Strum lightly over strings 3, 2 and 1 with a downward motion of your thumb or pick.

Study the illustration for the one-finger G7 chord. Do not play fingers 2 and 3 until later when you have mastered the simpler one-finger version. Strum across strings 4 through 1 with your thumb or pick.

When the chords are used as accompaniment to singing, they must be strummed with a steady, even stroke. Practice the following exercise strumming once for each chord letter or slash mark (**/**). Repeat this pattern several times.

C / / / / / / G7 / / / / / / /

Music is arranged into groups of beats or pulses. At the beginning of each song, you will see a number which tells you how many beats are in a group. Tap your foot to help keep a steady beat as you play and sing. Strum once on each beat. Now try this chord exercise with the C and G7 chords arranged in groups of four. Each group of four beats is separated by a vertical line called a **bar line**. Repeat this exercise several times.

4 C / / / | G7 / / / | C / / / | G7 / / / ‖

Now apply this strum to the songs on page 9.

Rock-A-My Soul

Rock - a - my soul in the bos - om of Ab - ra - ham,

Rock - a - my soul in the bos - om of Ab - ra - ham,

Rock - a - my soul in the bos - om of Ab - ra - ham,

Oh, rock - a - my soul! ___

He's Got The Whole World In His Hands

He's got the whole world___ in His hands,___ He's got the

whole world___ in His hands,___ He's got the whole world___

in His hands,___ He's got the whole world in His hands.___

Musical Symbols

Music is written in **notes** on a **staff.** The staff has five lines and four spaces between the lines. Where a note is written on the staff determines its **pitch** (highness or lowness). At the beginning of the staff is a **clef sign.** Guitar music is written in the treble clef.

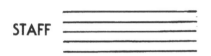

STAFF

TREBLE CLEF

Each line and space of the staff has a letter name: The **lines** are, (from bottom to top) E - G - B - D - F (which you can remember as Every Guitarist Begins Doing Fine): The spaces are from bottom to top, F - A - C - E, which spells "Face."

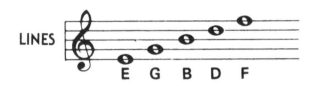

LINES

SPACES

The staff is divided into several parts by bar lines. The space between two bar lines is called a measure. To end a piece of music a double bar is placed on the staff.

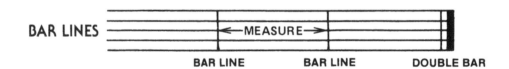

BAR LINES

BAR LINE   BAR LINE   DOUBLE BAR

Each measure contains a group of beats. Beats are the steady pulse of music. You respond to the pulse or beat when you tap your foot.

The two numbers placed next to the clef sign are the time signature. The top number tells you how many beats are in one measure.

TIME SIGNATURE

FOUR BEATS PER MEASURE
QUARTER NOTE (♩) GETS
ONE BEAT

Notes indicate the length (number of counts) of musical sound.

NOTES   WHOLE NOTE = 4 beats   HALF NOTE = 2 beats   QUARTER NOTE = 1 beat

The bottom number of the time signature tells you what kind of note will receive one beat. When different kinds of notes are placed on different lines or spaces, you will know the pitch of the note and how long to play the sound.

10

Notes on the First String

E **F** **G**

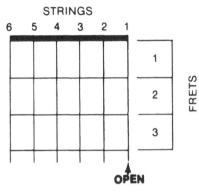

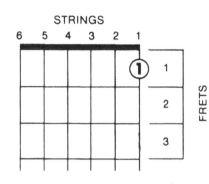

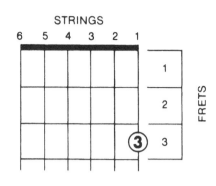

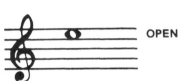

OPEN

1st FRET

1st FINGER

3rd FRET

3rd FINGER

Notes on the fourth space (E) of the staff are played on the open first string with no fingers depressed. The first string is the one closest to your knee.

Notes on the fifth line (F) of the staff are played by depressing the first string just behind the first fret. Use the tip of the first finger.

Notes on the space above the staff (G) are played by depressing the first string just behind the third fret. Use the third finger.

This sign (⊓) means to strike the string in a downward motion once for each note. After striking each note, let the sound ring for the full number of counts indicated. When playing a note with the string depressed (F or G), hold the left hand finger down for the duration of the note.

As you are playing, look ahead at the next note and get your fingers ready. Be sure to keep them just above the strings until you are ready to play the note. If they touch the string that is ringing, it will deaden the sound.

Always count and keep the beat steady. Practice each exercise until you play it well; then go on to the next exercise.

11

Exercises on the First String

At first practice the exercises slowly and steadily. When you can play them well at a slow speed, gradually increase the tempo (speed).

1   2   3   4

Touch only the tips of the fingers on the strings.

Keep the left hand fingers arched over the strings.

Some songs are longer than one line. When you reach the end of the first line of music, continue on to the second line without stopping.

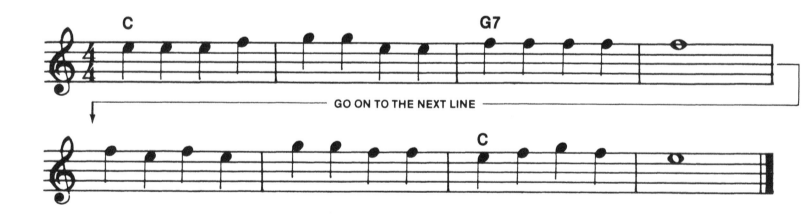

GO ON TO THE NEXT LINE

Review Of Music Symbols

1. Write the name and number of beats for each note:

$\frac{4}{4}$ ♩ = _____ beat(s)   𝅝 = _____ beat(s)   ♩ = _____ beat(s)

_____ **note**   _____ **note**   _____ **note**

2. Write the name for each music symbol below:

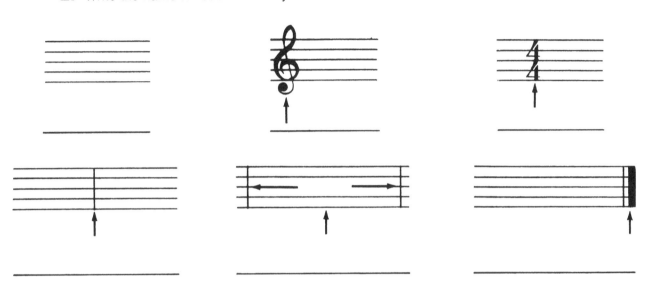

3. Write the letter names of the lines and spaces

SPACES   LINES

Write Your Own Music

Use the notes you know on the 1st string and compose a melody of your own. Use all three note values in the rhythm. Check to see that you have no more than 4 beats per measure. Write a treble clef sign and $\frac{4}{4}$ at the beginning and a treble clef on line 2.

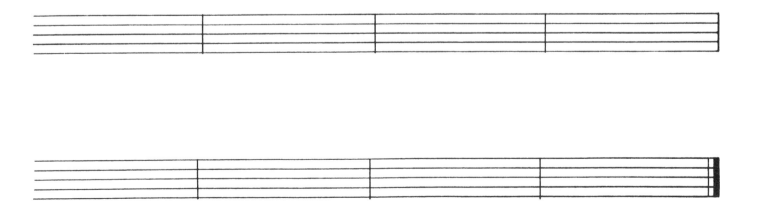

THE G CHORD

There are several ways to play the G chord. Begin by playing the one-finger version on strings 4 through 1; then add the 5th and 6th string fingers later for the full sound of these chords. The formation using fingers 2, 3 and 4 will seem more difficult at first, but it will be easier to move to the C and G7 chords and will pay dividends later.

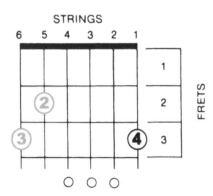 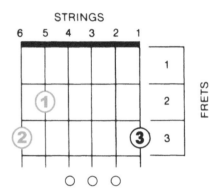

THE D7 CHORD

The D7 chord is a triangular formation of the fingers. You can play the full version of this chord right away. Arch your fingers so that the tips touch only one string each. Strum strings 4 through 1 for D7.

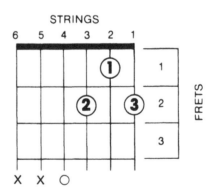

Now play these exercises using the G and D7 chords. The second exercise uses strums grouped in threes.

4 G / / / | **D7** / / / | G / / / | **D7** / / / ‖

3 G / / | **D7** / / | G / / | **D7** / / ‖

You are ready to play **Tom Dooley** in 4-beat groups and **Down In The Valley** in 3-beat groups.

14

Tom Dooley

Words and Music collected,
adapted and arranged by Frank Warner,
John A. Lomax and Alan Lomax

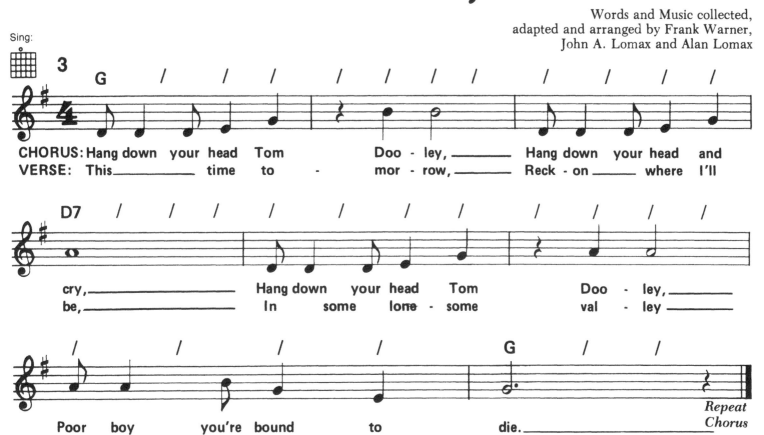

CHORUS: Hang down your head Tom Doo - ley, _____ Hang down your head and
VERSE: This _____ time to - mor - row, _____ Reck - on _____ where I'll

cry, _____ Hang down your head Tom Doo - ley, _____
be, _____ In some lone - some val - ley _____

Poor boy you're bound to die. _____
hang - ing from a white oak tree. _____

Repeat Chorus

Down In The Valley

Down in the val - ley, _____ Val - ley so
Hear the wind blow _____ dear, _____ Hear the wind

low, _____ Hang your head o -
blow, _____

ver, _____ Hear the wind blow. _____

15

Notes on the Second String

B

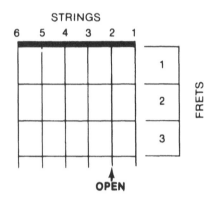

OPEN

OPEN

Notes on the third line (B) of the staff are played on the open second string with no fingers depressed.

C

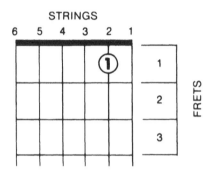

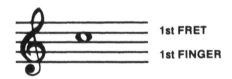

1st FRET

1st FINGER

Notes on the third space (C) of the staff are played by depressing the second string just behind the first fret. Use the tip of the first finger.

D

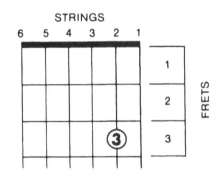

3rd FRET

3rd FINGER

Notes on the fourth line (D) of the staff are played by depressing the second string just behind the third fret. Use the third finger.

Always count out loud as you play and give each note its full value. Keep the beat steady. Now try the exercises below. Remember to practice each exercise until you can play it well; then go on to the next exercise.

COUNT: 1 - 2 - 3 - 4   1 - 2 - 3 - 4   1 - 2 - 3 - 4   1 - 2 - 3 - 4   1 - 2 - 3 - 4

1 - 2   3 - 4   1 - 2   3 - 4   1 - 2   3 - 4   1 - 2   3 - 4   1 - 2 - 3 - 4

1   2   3   4   1   2   3   4   1   2   3   4   1   2   3   4   1 - 2 - 3 - 4

16

Exercises on the Second String

Always practice the exercises slowly and steadily at first. After you can play them well at a slower tempo, gradually increase the speed. If some of your notes are fuzzy or unclear, move your left hand finger slightly until you get a clear sound.

Moving from String to String

You have learned six notes now, three on the first string and three on the second string. In the following exercises you will be moving from string to string. As you are playing one note, look ahead to the next and get your fingers in position.

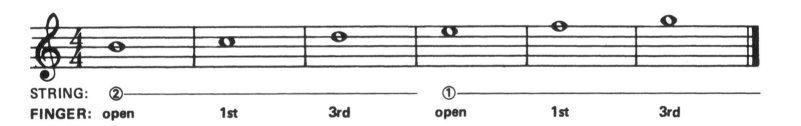

STRING:	②			①		
FINGER:	open	1st	3rd	open	1st	3rd

2-STRING ALTERNATION

17

On your first songs, strum marks / were given above the music to guide you in your first stage of development. Once you understand that you should strum with a steady stroke on every beat of the measure, these marks become unnecessary.

The next two songs use the G, C and D7 chords you already know. Strum on each beat of the measure. Keep your right hand steady.

This Little Light Of Mine

SING AND STRUM

```
        G
2. Everywhere I go, I'm gonna let it shine,
   C                              G
   Everywhere I go, I'm gonna let it shine,

   Everywhere I go, I'm gonna let it shine,

                 D7        G
   Let it shine, let it shine, let it shine.


        G
3. We've got the light of freedom, we're gonna let it shine,
   C                                          G
   We've got the light of freedom, we're gonna let it shine,

   We've got the light of freedom, we're gonna let it shine,

                 D7        G
   Let it shine, let it shine, let it shine.
```

The song, **Do Lord,** uses this same tune and chords.

18

Down By The Riverside begins with an incomplete measure — three notes called **pick-up notes.** Sing the first words, "I'm gonna"; then begin strumming the steady beat where you see the G chord symbol.

Down By The Riverside

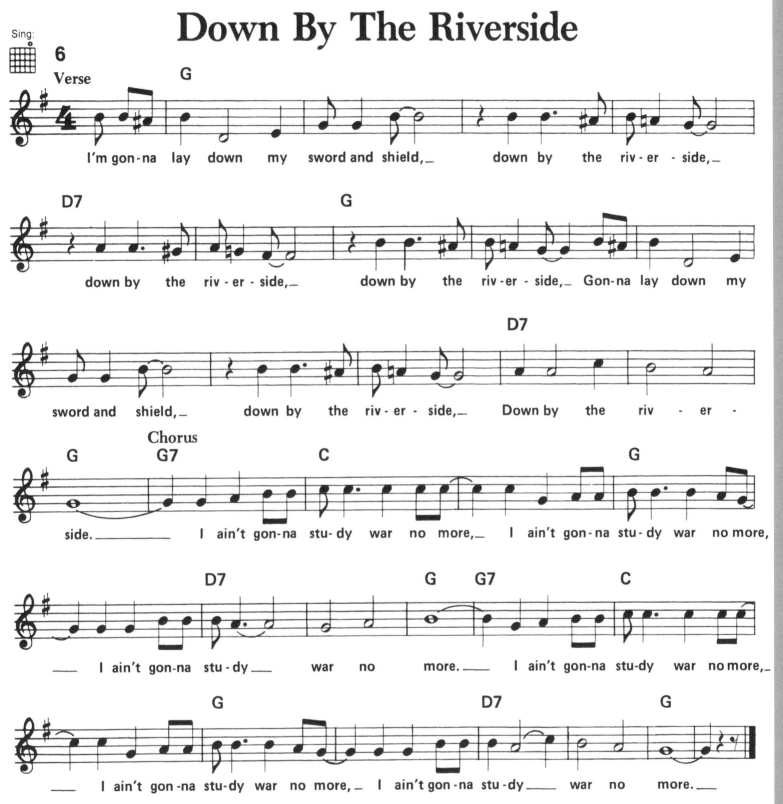

2. **Gonna shake hands around the world, down by the riverside,**
   D7   G
   Down by the riverside, down by the riverside,
   Gonna shake hands around the world, down by the riverside,
   D7   G
   Down by the riverside. *CHORUS*

Melodies on Strings 1 and 2

Practice these familiar songs played on strings 1 and 2. Always begin slowly and then gradually increase the tempo.

Gray chord symbols are used throughout the book to indicate that the chords should be played by the instructor.

ODE TO JOY

Germany

AUNT RHODY

Go, tell Aunt Rho - dy, Go, tell Aunt Rho - dy,

Go, tell Aunt Rho - dy the old grey goose is dead.

SKIP TO MY LOU

Lost my part - ner, what'll I do? Lost my part - ner, what'll I do?

Lost my part - ner, what'll I do? Skip to my Lou my dar - ling.

Guitar Ensemble

A guitar ensemble (group) is a piece which features several guitars playing different parts at the same time. The first example below is written in the form of a **round.** Follow this plan to play the round:

- Play the entire piece (3 lines) twice through in unison to learn it.
- Split the class into four equal sections. Number the groups 1 through 4.
- Group 1 begins at the beginning and plays the piece twice through.
- Group 2 starts at the beginning when group 1 reaches the second line (asterisk ✱).
- Group 3 starts at the beginning when group 2 reaches the second line.
- Group 4 strums the chords above the line.
- All groups play twice through the piece.

'ROUND ABOUT

Write Your Own Music

Using the notes you have learned, write your own piece of music. Write the music in such a way that the last note is third-space C. Write a treble clef sign at the beginning of each line and a double bar at the end. Tape record the melody or have a friend play it while you try playing the C and G7 chords with it.

STRUM VARIATIONS

Up to this point you have strummed with a downward stroke on each beat of the measure. This simple strum will continue to prove useful on songs where you want an uncomplicated accompaniment.

You can vary this basic strum by adding an UP STROKE after each DOWN STROKE. This DOWN/UP STRUM will seem like it is moving twice as fast, because you will be playing a down/up stroke on each beat.

⊓ is the sign for a down stroke.   ∨ is the sign for an up stroke.

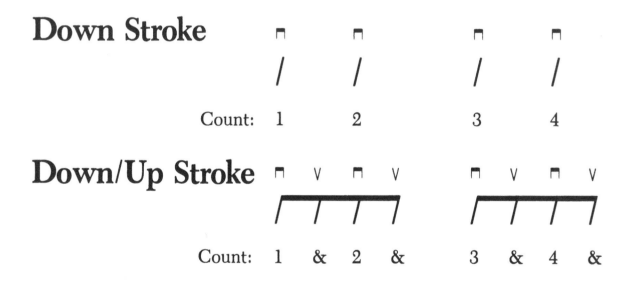

The down/up strum can be played three different ways:

1. A PICK held in the right hand (a louder and "harder" sound)

2. The fleshy right-hand THUMB plays both down and up strokes (a softer sound)

3. The nail of the INDEX FINGER plays the down (brush) stroke, and the nail of the THUMB plays the up stroke. (a harder, louder sound like the pick)

   NOTE: Keep the fingers and thumb relaxed and rotate the wrist. This strum alternates well with finger picking introduced later in the book.

Try all three ways of playing. A good player will use different right-hand strums to achieve different effects for the style of each song.

Play this strumming exercise on the chords you already know:

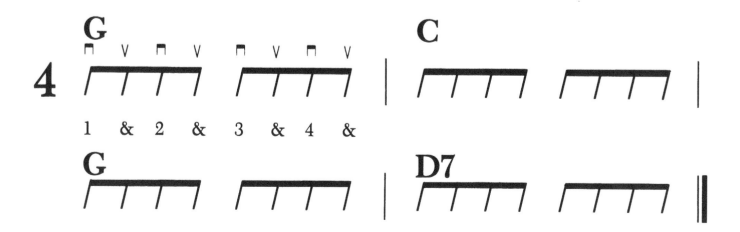

Now play the down/up strum on Elvis Presley's rock hit, **Hound Dog**.

Hound Dog

Words and Music by
Jerry Leiber and Mike Stoller

Keep the common 1st finger down when moving from D7 to C.

Hound Dog is one of many early rock 'n' roll hits which uses the form of **12-Bar Blues** borrowed from the black blues tradition. You will return to the blues later in this book on page 87.

If you have not yet learned to play the full G, C and G7 chords, you might wish to return to page 8 and review this material. If you are not ready to play these fuller chords at this time, don't worry; you can always return to these chords at a later point.

Notes on the Third String

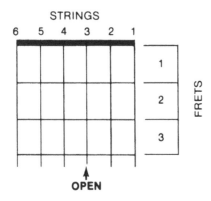

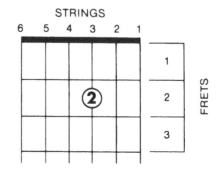

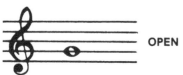

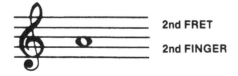

Notes on the second line (G) of the staff are played on the open third string.

Notes on the second space (A) of the staff are played by depressing the third string just behind the second fret.

Keep the fingers arched over the strings at all times so they will be in position to finger the next note.

Using Strings 2 and 3

The following exercises use the five notes you can play on strings 2 and 3. Practice each line slowly and carefully until you can play it with ease.

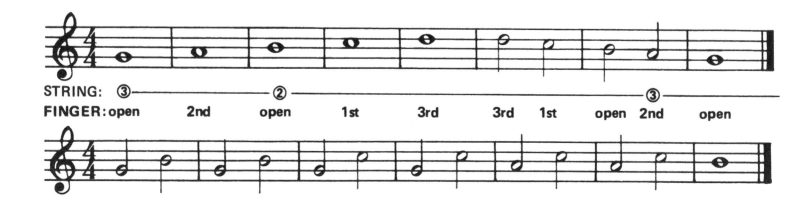

Strings 1, 2, and 3

STRING: ③——————————②————————————————————①——————
FINGER: open   2nd   open   1st   3rd   open   1st   3rd

YANKEE DOODLE

12

OLD JOE CLARK

13

American Fiddle Tune

THE CAPO

Metal Capo **Elastic Capo**

One of the advantages of using a capo is that you can move a song to a vocal range that is comfortable for your voice. The capo also allows you to use easier chords for playing certain songs.

When you use a capo, place it as close to the fret wire as you can. This will help to eliminate string buzzing. If you have considerable warping on your guitar neck, you may find the capo somewhat difficult to use effectively.

On the following page the new song, **Eleanor Rigby**, is pitched in a high singing key where it was sung by the Beatles. The chords are easy to play in this key, so it is written very much like the original version. If you want to sing in a lower, more comfortable key, you can capo at the 5th fret and sing lower. The starting singing pitch is given for use with or without the capo.

THE Em CHORD

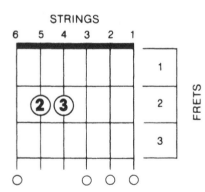

The Em chord is one of the easiest chords on the guitar. Arch your fingers and play on the tips to avoid touching the other open strings.

After you have played through **Eleanor Rigby** using a simple down strum on each beat, try this new variation on the down/up strum:

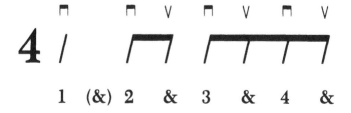

Let the first-beat strum ring for a full beat. Follow the down ⊓ and up V strokes carefully.

Eleanor Rigby

Words and Music by
John Lennon and Paul McCartney

Sing:

14

Option: Capo 5
and sing lower

Ah_____ look at all_____ the lone - ly peo - ple!_____

1. E - lea - nor Rig - by, picks up the rice in the church where a wed - ding has been,__
2. Fath-er Mc-Ken - zie, writ-ing the words of a ser - mon that no___ one will hear,__
3. E - lea - nor Rig - by, died in the church and was bur - ied a - long__ with her name,__

_____ lives in a dream._____ Waits at the win - dow,
_____ no one comes near._____ Look at him work - ing,
_____ no - bod - y came._____ Fath- er Mç - ken - zie,

wear-ing the face____ that she keeps____ in a jar____ by the door,_____
darn-ing his socks____ in the night____ when there's no - bod - y there,_____
wip -ing the dirt____ from his hands____ as he walks__ from the grave,_____

who is it for?_____
what does he care?_____ All the lone - ly peo - ple, where
no one was saved._____

do they all___ come from?_____ All the lone - ly peo -

- ple, where do they all___ be - long?_____

D.C. al Fine
after 3rd Verse

Sing and Strum

Repeat Sign :‖

The double bar line with two dots :‖ tells you to repeat a section of music. Two repeat signs ‖: :‖ tell you to repeat the music between them.

D.C. al Fine

"D.C. (Da Capo) al Fine" tells you to go back to the beginning and play until you reach the Fine (end).

Guitar Ensemble

A duet is a song that has two parts that can be played together. Practice both parts of the following duet. Ask your instructor or a friend to play the duet with you. If you have a tape recorder, you can record one of the parts and then play a duet with yourself. A third part can be added by strumming the chords.

AU CLAIR DE LA LUNE

France

AURA LEE

16

Some music has three beats per measure instead of four. This is indicated by the top number of the time signature.

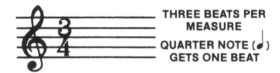

THREE BEATS PER MEASURE

QUARTER NOTE (♩) GETS ONE BEAT

Remember that the bottom number tells you what kind of note gets one beat.

When a dot is added to a note, the value of the note increases by one-half. Since a half note (♩) gets two beats, a dotted half note (♩.) gets two beats plus one beat or three beats.

EXERCISE IN 3/4 TIME

HE'S A JOLLY GOOD FELLOW

England

17

He's a jol-ly good fel - low, For he's a jol-ly good

fel - low, For he's a jol - ly good fel - -

low, Which no-bod-y can ____ de - ny.

29

Tell Ol' Bill and **Where Have All The Flowers Gone?** will give you good practice at combining the Em chord with chords you already know. When you have played the chords to the songs using a simple strum and feel comfortable with your left-hand changes, use the new variation on the down/up strum as an accompaniment.

Tell Ol' Bill

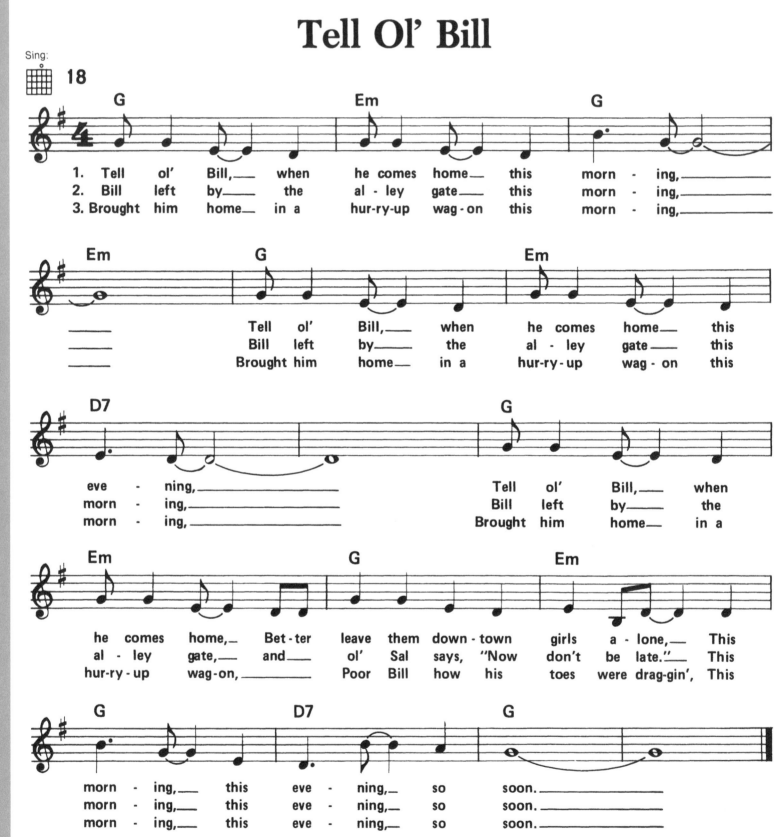

Go back and learn the full C, G and G7 chords as soon as your hand size and progress permit.

Where Have All The Flowers Gone?

Sing

19

Option: Capo 3

Words and Music by
Pete Seeger

Where have all the flow-ers gone?__ long time pass - ing, __ Where have all the flow-ers gone?__ long time a - go, Where have all the flow-ers gone?__ Young girls picked them ev - 'ry one, __ When will they ev - er learn?__ When will they ev - er learn? _____

2. Where have all the young girls gone? long time passing,
   Where have all the young girls gone? long time ago,
   Where have all the young girls gone? Gone to young men everyone,
   When will they ever learn? When will they ever learn?

3. Where have all the young men gone? long time passing,
   Where have all the young men gone? long time ago,
   Where have all the young men gone? Gone to soldiers everyone,
   When will they ever learn? When will they ever learn?

4. Where have all the soldiers gone? long time passing, (2)
   Where have all the soldiers gone? Gone to graveyards, everyone. etc.

5. Where have all the graveyards gone? long time passing, (2)
   Where have all the graveyards gone? Gone to flowers, everyone. etc.

SING AND STRUM

Reading 3-String Chords

In this section you will learn to read the notes for chords you already know. These chords will then be used in the solos on the next pages.

Study the illustrations below and practice each chord. Strike the strings one, two, and three with one downward motion.

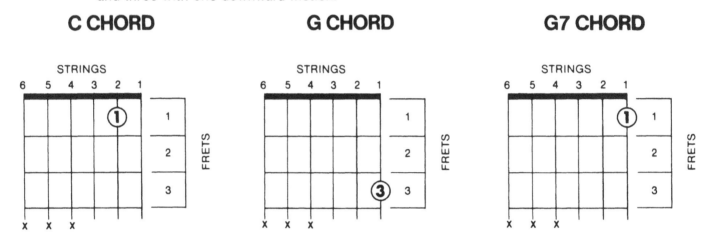

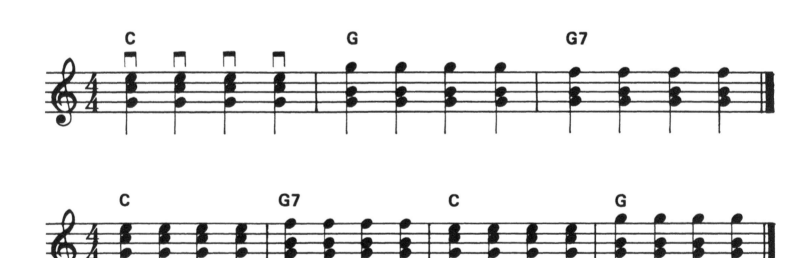

Practice writing out the three chords above in stacked half notes.

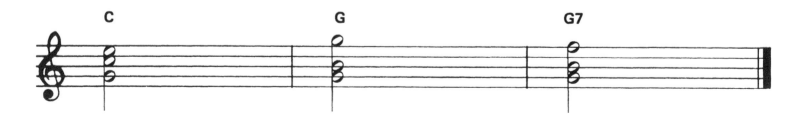

Guitar Solos

You have been playing either the melody or the chord strums in the previous exercises. Now combine the chords and the melody. First, play through the melodies (the top notes only). When you feel you know the melodies well enough, strum each chord. Finally, combine the melody and the chords. Practice the exercise slowly and steadily and gradually increase the tempo as you progress.

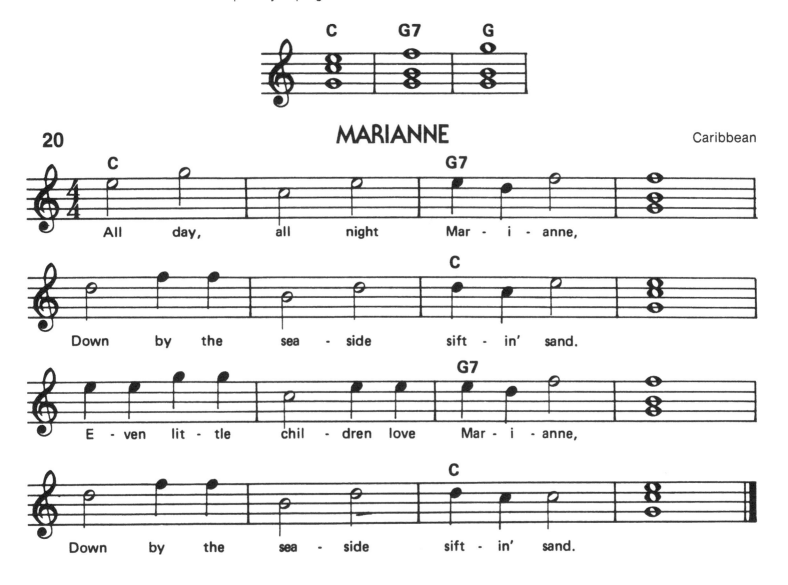

20   MARIANNE   Caribbean

Remember to practice the melody (top notes only) and then strum the chords before combining them.

WHEN I NEED YOU

Words by Carole Bayer Sager
Music by Albert Hammond.

Review Of Music Symbols

1. Write the letter names and string numbers for the notes below:

Letter: <u>F</u> __ __ __ __ __ __

String: <u>1</u> __ __ __ __ __ __

2. Write the counts below the music.

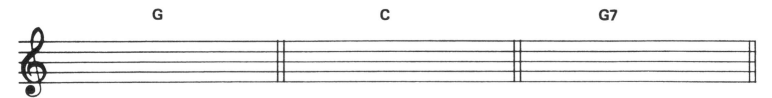

3. Write the correct stack of three notes for each of these 3-string chords:

Write (Improvise) Your Own Music

When a melody is combined with chords **(harmony)**, the melody uses notes from the chords on the strong beats (1 and 3) of each measure. Notes not found in the chords **(non-chord tones)** can be used on the weaker beats (2 and 4).

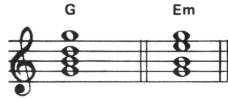

- Study the notes above that make up the G and Em chords.
- Tape record or have another guitarist (half of the class) play the chordal background.
- Play the first-line sample melody over the chords; then continue playing (**improvising** or making up) your own melody.
- After you have improvised for some time, write down a melody that fits with the chords.

35

THE SYNCOPATED STRUM

Syncopation is defined as off-beat rhythm or the accenting of notes that fall on the & between counts. The syncopated strums so vital to popular music today are a result of the unique blend of African rhythms and European and Latin American musical elements.

Practice the syncopated strums below as a variation on the down/up strum:

• Establish the down/up strum pattern until you can do it without thinking.

• Continue this down/up action throughout the syncopated strums, but "miss" the strings with a silent stroke where you see the word "miss."

• This will result in the desired rhythms and will allow you to easily shift back and forth from one strum to another.

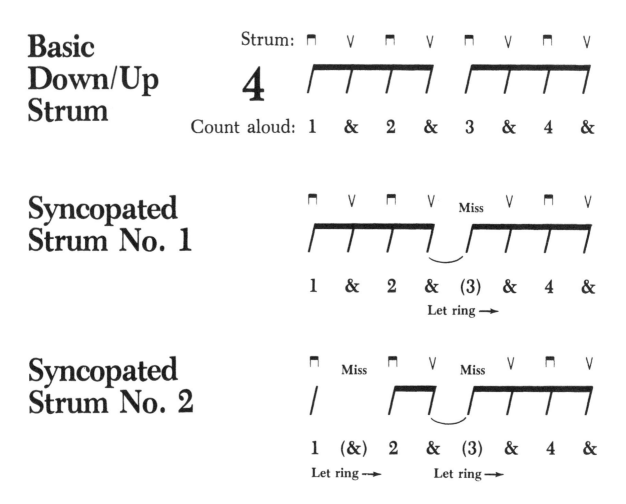

Play the following sequence of chords with each of the syncopated strums above. First, begin with four strum patterns per chord; then decrease the number until you are playing one strum pattern per chord. Tap your foot or play with a metronome to establish a steady rhythm. These strums must be automatic in order to sing with them.

G	Em	G	D7
G	C	D7	G

Before you play the syncopated strums with **The Midnight Special**, go back and apply them to **Hound Dog, Tell Ol' Bill** or **Where Have All The Flowers Gone?**

The Midnight Special

Words and Music by Huddie Ledbetter
Collected and Adapted by
John A. Lomax and Alan Lomax

Sing:

22

G | **C**
Well you wake up in the morn - ing, _____ hear the ding - dong

G | **D7**
ring, _____ Go march-ing to the ta - ble, _____ see the same damn

G | **C** | **G**
thing, Knife and fork are on the ta - ble _____ noth-in' in my pan, _____

D7 | **G**
_____ And if you say a thing a - bout it, _____ you're in trou-ble with the man.

Chorus

C | **G**
Let the mid - night spe - cial, _____ shine its light on _____ you. _____

D7 | **G**
_____ Let the mid - night spe - cial shine its ev - er lov-in' light on _____ you. _____

Sing and Strum

    G   **C**   **G**
2.   If you ever go to Houston, you better walk right,

    D7   **G**
You better not stagger and you better not fight,

    C   **G**
Or the sheriff will arrest you, he will carry you down.

    D7   **G**
If the jury finds you guilty, you're penitentiary bound. *CHORUS*

37

Notes on the Fourth String

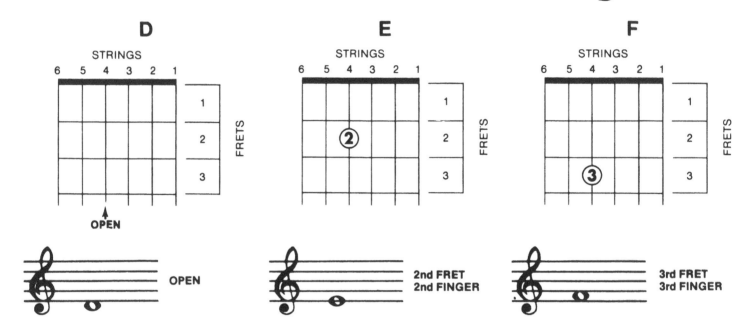

D	E	F
OPEN	2nd FRET / 2nd FINGER	3rd FRET / 3rd FINGER

Practice each exercise carefully. Remember to keep your fingers arched over the strings.

1 - 2 - 3 - 4

Using Strings 2, 3, and 4

Try these exercises which use the second, third, and fourth strings. Watch for the G chord in the last measure of each exercise.

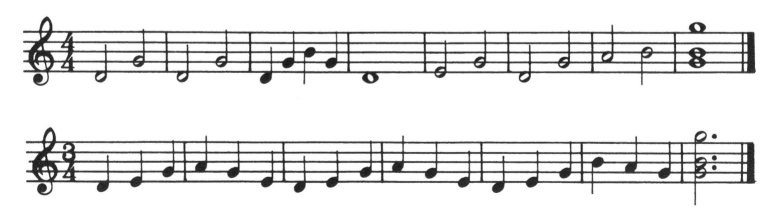

TRY TO REMEMBER

Words by Tom Jones
Music by Harvey Schmidt

2-BEAT STRUMS

Until now the chords and strums that you have used have all lasted at least four beats or one measure. Sometimes, however, chords change every two beats, and strums that last four beats will not work. At that point, you should switch to a two-beat strum like one of those below:

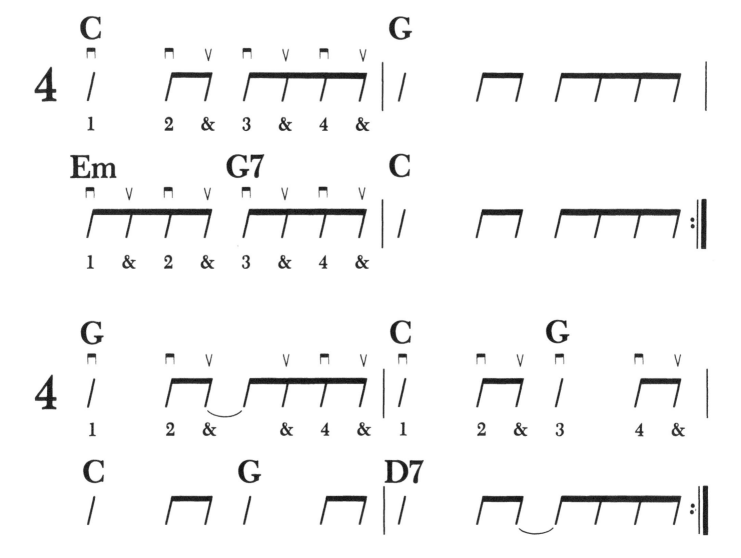

Playing the two-beat strums in isolation is easy, but switching between two- and four-beat strums will take careful practice. Your greatest help will come from maintaining a steady down/up stroke with variations provided by missing the strings with a silent stroke. Practice the following exercises that will help you make the transitions from four beats to two beats:

Develop your ability to play the strums with your fingers or with a pick (See page 14.)

Scout your way through **If I Had A Hammer** to find the two-beat chords where your strum must change.

Use a combination of ⌐⌐V V⌐V and ⌐⌐V ⌐⌐V on this piece.

If I Had A Hammer
(The Hammer Song)

Words and Music by
Lee Hays and Pete Seeger

Sing:
24

Option: Capo 3
and sing lower

1. If I had a ham - mer, I'd ham - mer in the
2. If I had a bell, I'd ring it in the

morn - ing, I'd ham - mer in the eve - ning
morn - ing, I'd ring it in the eve - ning

all o - ver this land, I'd ham - mer out
all o - ver this land, I'd ring out

dan - ger, I'd ham - mer out a warn - ing,
dan - ger, I'd ring out a warn - ing,

I'd ham - mer out love be - tween my broth-ers and my sis - ters,
I'd ring out love be - tween my broth-ers and my sis - ters,

all o - ver this land.
all o - ver this land.

3. If I had a song, I'd sing it in the morning,
   I'd sing it in the evening all over this land,
   I'd sing out danger, I'd sing out a warning,
   I'd sing about love between my brothers and my sisters,
   All over this land.

4. Well, I've got a hammer, and I've got a bell,
   And I've got a song to sing all over this land,
   It's the hammer of justice, It's the bell of freedom,
   It's the song about love between my brothers and my sisters,
   All over this land.

Sing and Strum

Pickup Notes

Music doesn't always begin on beat one. When you begin after beat one, the notes before the first full measure are called pickup notes. The following illustrations show several examples of pickup notes. Count the missing beats out loud before you begin playing.

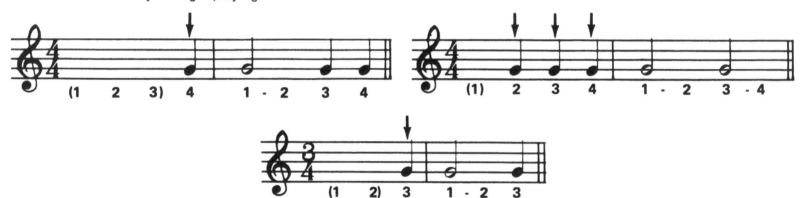

THE RIDDLE SONG

British

When a song begins with pickup notes, the last measure will be short the exact number of beats used as pickups.

TIES

A curved line which connects two notes of the same pitch is called a tie. The first note is struck and held for the value of both notes. The second note should not be played again. Look at the following illustration of tied notes.

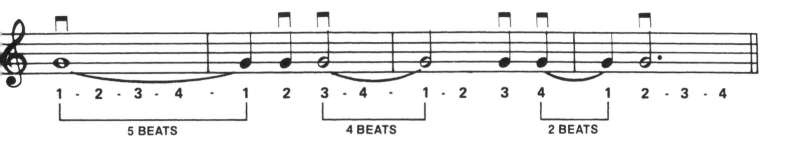

Practice the following melody carefully. When you can play it well, sing and strum the chords. Remember to strum one chord on each beat of a measure.

THIS LAND IS YOUR LAND

Words and Music by
Woody Guthrie

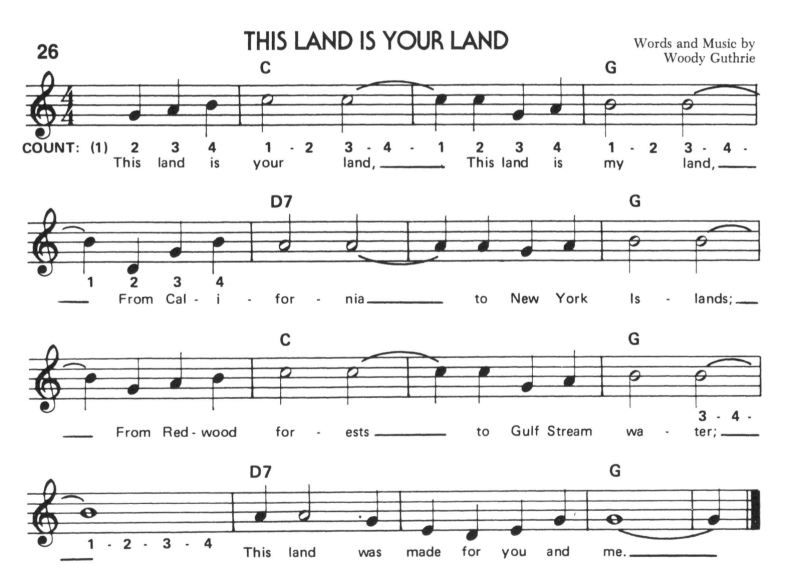

AMAZING GRACE

A - maz - ing Grace, How sweet the sound, That
saved a wretch like me; _____ I once was lost, but
now am found; Was blind, but now I see. _____

COMIN' THROUGH THE RYE

Scotland

CARNIVAL OF VENICE

Italy

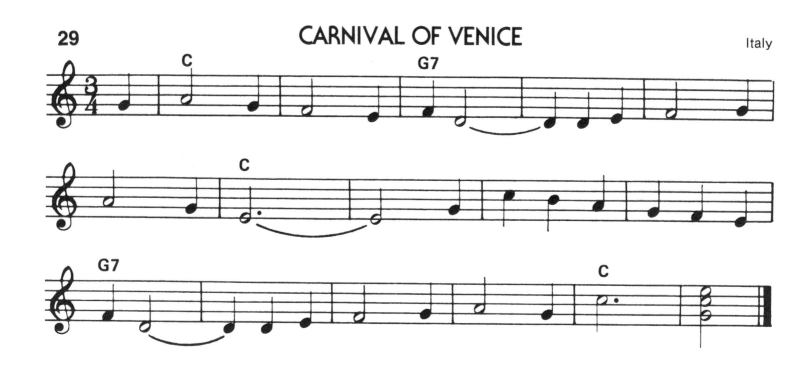

Guitar Ensemble

Play the 3- and 4-part rounds which follow by dividing into groups. Follow the same procedure as on page 21. Group 2 begins when Group 1 reaches the asterisk *, and so on. Play once in unison and twice as a round.

4-PART ROUND

30

3-PART ROUND

31

4-PART ROUND

32

THE D AND A7 CHORDS

D

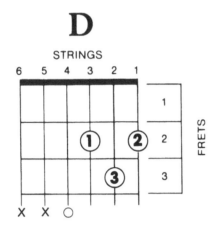

A7

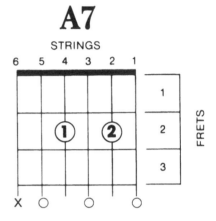

The D chord is a triangular shaped chord pointing toward the body of the guitar. Arch your fingers, and keep your thumb in back of the neck. Play strings 4 through 1.

The A7 chord is easily moved to and from the D chord. Consider fingers 1 and 2 as a unit and move them back and forth together. Arch your fingers so that strings 3 and 1 are not dampened. Play strings 5 through 1.

Practice the following chord changes using any of the four- and two-beat strum patterns you already know. Keep a steady beat with your toe or a metronome. Get to the new chord on time even if it means leaving the old chord a bit early. Try to move your fingers to a new chord as a **unit** instead of "letting your fingers do the walking" one at a time.

4 D / / / | / / / / | A7 / / / | / / / / |

G / / / | A7 / / / | D / / / | / / / / ‖

4 D / / / | A7 / / / | D / A7 / | D / A7 / |

Em / / / | G / A7 / | D / G / | D / / / ‖

Now go back to page 9 and replay the two-chord songs, **Rock-A-My Soul** and **He's Got The Whole World In His Hand,** substituting the D chord for C and the A7 chord for G7. This process is called **transposition.**

Colours

Words and Music by
Donovan

Sing:

33

Option: Capo 2 or 3

1. Yel-low is the col-our of my true love's hair
2. Blue is the col-our of the sky a-bove
} In the

morn-ing _____ when we rise, _____ In the

morn-ing _____ when we rise _____ That's the time, _____

_____ that's the time _____ I love the best. _____

SING AND STRUM

3. Green is the colour of the sparkling corn (or Douglas Fir) in the morning...

4. White is the colour of the new-fall'n snow in the morning...

5. Freedom is a word that I seldom use without thinking, mm_____,
   Without thinking mm_____ of the time,
   Of the time when we first loved.

6. (Make up your own new verses) or repeat verse 1.

A Place In The Choir

Words and Music by
Bill Staines

Sing:
34
Option: Capo 2 or 3

Chorus

All God's crit-ters got a place in the choir. Some sing low,

some sing high-er, Some sing out loud on the tel-e-phone wire,

Some just clap their hands or paws or an-y-thing they got now._____

Verse

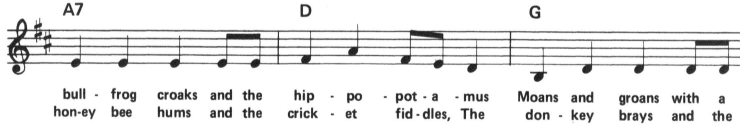

1. Lis-ten to the bass, it's the one on the bot-tom Where the
(2.) dogs_____ and the cats_____ they_____ take up the mid-dle While the

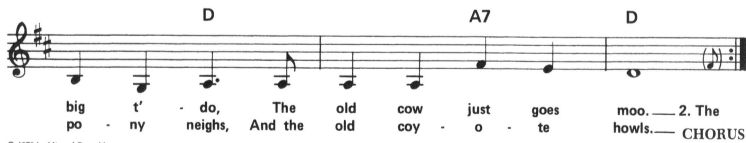

bull-frog croaks and the hip-po-pot-a-mus Moans and groans with a
hon-ey bee hums and the crick-et fid-dles, The don-key brays and the

big t'-do, The old cow just goes moo.____ 2. The
po-ny neighs, And the old coy-o-te howls.____ CHORUS

3. **Listen to the top where the little birds sing**
   On the melodies with the high notes ringing,
   The hoot owl hollers over everything
   And the jaybird disagrees.

4. **Singin' in the night time, singin' in the day,**
   The little duck quacks, then he's on his way,
   The possum ain't got much to say,
   And the porcupine talks to himself. *CHORUS*

5. **It's a simple song of living sung everywhere**
   By the ox and the fox and the grizzly bear,
   The grumpy alligator and the hawk above,
   The sly raccoon and the turtle dove. *CHORUS*

SING AND STRUM

THE BASS NOTE/AFTER STRUM

The next stage of development for your right hand is to learn the bass note/after strum technique. The nature of this accompaniment pattern is:

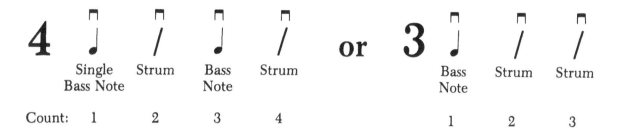

The bass note/after strum can be played in several different ways:

1. With a **pick** — Play a single bass string; then strum lightly downward across the remaining treble strings.

2. With the **thumb** — Pluck a single bass string with the thumb; then strum downward across the remaining treble strings with the fleshy part of the thumb.

3. With the **thumb and fingers** — Pluck a single bass note with the thumb; then strum downward across the treble strings with the fingernail of the index (and middle) fingers(s).

Playing the proper bass string for each chord will take some practice. Below is a chart showing the correct bass string number for each of the chords you know:

Chords:	A7	C	D or D7	Em	G or G7
Bass String:	5	5	4	6	6

Practice the following bass note/after strum exercise which indicates the string number for each bass note and a slash mark for the after strum:

$\frac{4}{}$

D				A7			
4 /	4 /	4 /	4 /	5 /	5 /	5 /	5 /

G		Em		A7		D	
6 /	6 /	6 /	6 /	5 /	5 /	4 /	4 / :‖

When you can play these patterns with ease, go back to **A Place in the Choir** and **Colours** and apply the bass note/after strum technique to these pieces.

Practice the three-beat exercise below before going on to **Goodnight Irene**:

$\frac{3}{}$

D	D7	G	
4 / /	4 / /	6 / /	6 / /

Em	A7	D	
6 / /	5 / /	4 / /	4 / / :‖

Goodnight Irene

Words and Music by
Huddie Ledbetter and John A. Lomax

Sing:

35

Option: Capo 2 or 3

SING AND STRUM

Chorus

I - rene, good - night,_____ I -

rene, good - night._____ Good - night, I - rene, good -

night, I - rene, I'll see you in my dreams._____

Fine

2. Last
3. Stop

Verse

1. Some - times I live in the coun - try,_____
(2.) Sat - ur - day night I got mar - ried,_____
(3.) ram - blin',_____ stop your gam - blin',_____ Stop

Some - times I live in town._____ Now
Me and my wife set - tled down._____ Go
stay - in' out late at night._____

Some - times I get a great no - tion_____ to
me and my wife_____ are part - ed,_____ Gonna
home to your wife_____ and fam - 'ly,_____ Sit

D.C. al Fine

jump in the riv - er and drown._____
take an - oth - er stroll_____ down town._____
down by the fire - side bright._____

Notes on the Fifth String

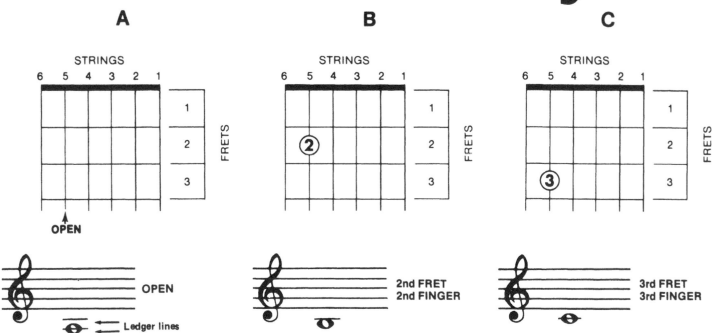

A **B** **C**

LEDGER LINES Ledger lines extend the range of the staff by continuing the alternation of spaces and lines using the musical alphabet (A through G).

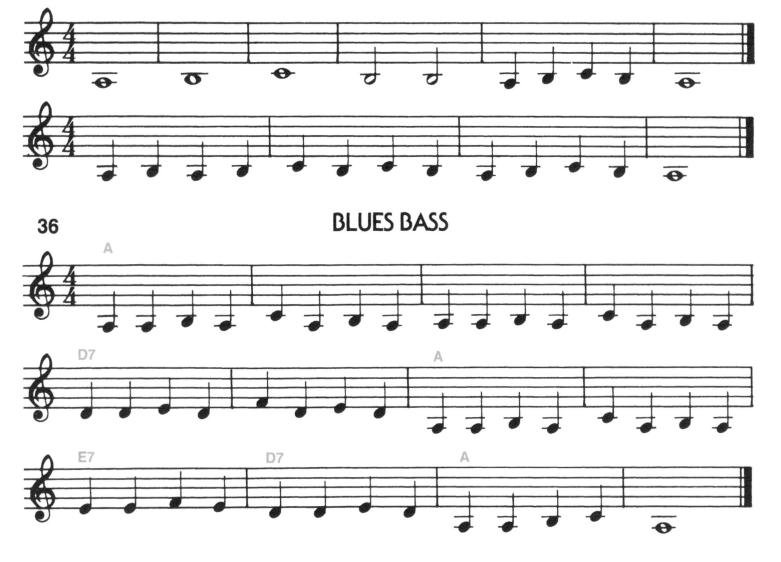

36 **BLUES BASS**

NINE POUND HAMMER

Words and Music by
Merle Travis

37

This nine pound ham- mer_____ is a little too heav- y_____
_____ For my size,_____ Honey, for my size._____
_____ I'm goin' on the moun- tain_____ gonna see my Ba- by_____
_____ But I ain't comin' back,_____ I ain't comin' back._____
_____ Roll on Bud- dy,_____ don't roll so slow._____
_____ How can I roll_____ when the wheels won't go?_____
_____ Roll on Bud- dy,_____ pull a load of coal._____
_____ How can I pull_____ when the wheels don't roll?_____

Practice these familiar melodies until you feel comfortable playing them. Remember to look ahead as you play so you can prepare for the next notes.

THE VOLGA BOATMAN

38   Russia

GREENSLEEVES

39   England

A - las, my love,____ you do me wrong ____ to

cast me off____ dis - court - eous - ly, When I have

loved _____ you so long ____ de - light - ing in your

com - pa - ny. Green - sleeves ____ was all my joy, _____

Green - - sleeves was my de - light, Green - sleeves was my

heart of gold,____ and who ____ but la - dy Green - sleeves.

Guitar Ensemble

A **rest** is a musical symbol for silence. There are different types of rests for each note value. Continue counting through rests, but do not play.

$\frac{4}{4}$ 𝄽 = **Quarter Rest** (1 beat)   ▬ = **Half Rest** (2 beats)   ▬ = **Whole Rest** (4 beats)

Observe the rests as you play the duet below. The teacher or more advanced students will play the background chords. Divide the class into two groups.

BY THE TIME I GET TO PHOENIX

Words and Music by
Jim Webb

THE Am CHORD

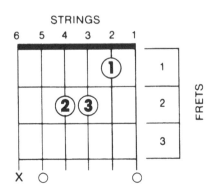

STRINGS
6 5 4 3 2 1

FRETS

The Am chord should be played from strings 5 through 1. The 5th string should be played as the bass string. Be careful not to lean on the first string and dampen it with your 1st finger.

Play this series of chord changes to become acquainted with Am. First, use any of the strum patterns you already know; then repeat the exercises with the bass note/after strum technique.

Hold down any common fingers between two chords For example, note that the Am and C chords have a common 1st and 2nd finger. Keep these fingers down when changing chords.

4 Am / / / | / / / / | C / / / | / / / / |
   Em / / / | G / / / | Am / / / | / / / / :|

4 C / / / | Am / / / | Em / / / | G / / / |
   Am / Em / | Am / C / | Am / G / | C / / / :|

Use a simple strum while learning the chords to **Sixteen Tons**; then try the bass note/after strum to accompany your singing.

Sixteen Tons

Sing: 41

Words and Music by
Merle Travis

Verse   Em

1. Some   peo - ple   say   a   man   is   made   out   of   mud___   A
2. (I was)   born___ one___   morn - in' when the sun   did - n't   shine___   I
3. (I was)   born___ one___   morn - in', it   was driz - zl - ing   rain_____
4. (If you)   see_____ me _____ com - in' bet - ter____   step a - side___   A

The symbol ⌒ is called a **fermata**; and it tells you to **hold** a note.

The brackets over the last line are called **endings**. Play the 1, 2, 3 ending after verses 1, 2 and 3 repeating back to the beginning. On verse 4 skip over the 1, 2, 3 and play the 4 ending.

Notes on the Sixth String

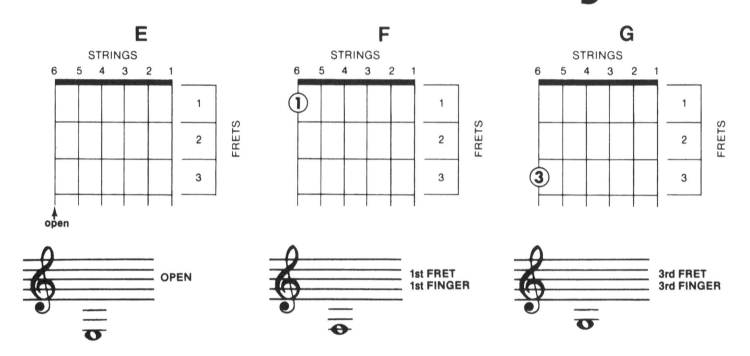

Always practice slowly and steadily at first; then gradually increase the tempo:

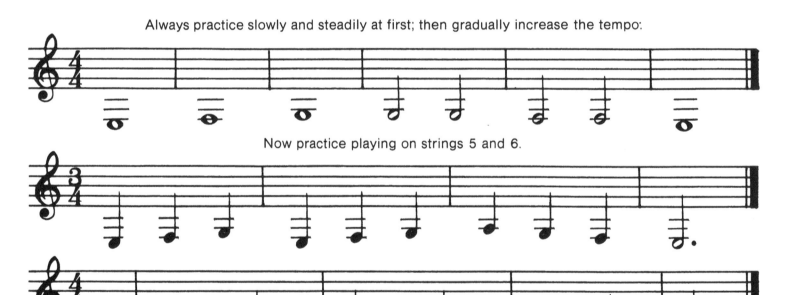

Now practice playing on strings 5 and 6.

The following exercise will give you the opportunity to practice the notes on strings 2, 3, 4, 5, and 6. Look ahead as you play so you can prepare for the next note.

BUTTERMILK HILL

Ireland

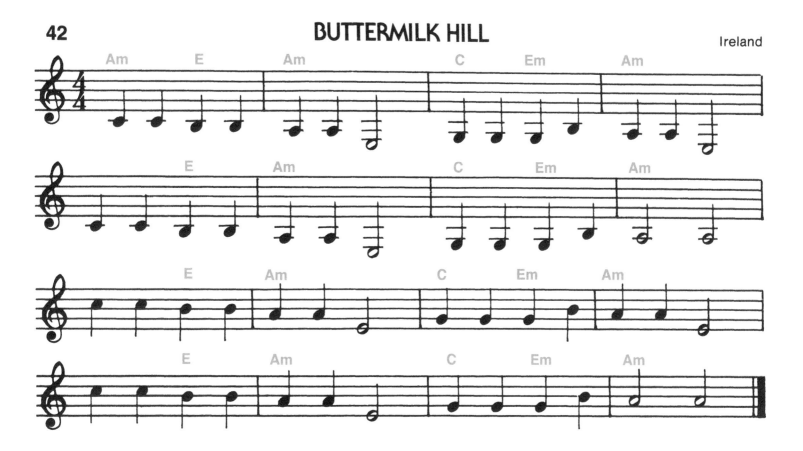

The interval between notes that have the same letter name and are eight notes apart is called an octave. The second half of Buttermilk Hill is written one octave higher than the first half.

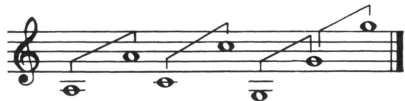

THE FROG WENT COURTIN'

43

The frog went court-in', he did ride, uh - huh, The frog went court-in',

he did ride, uh huh, The frog went court - in', he did ride with

sword and pis - tols by his side, uh, huh, huh, huh.

REVIEW OF MUSIC SYMBOLS

1. Write the letter name below each note.

_ _ _ _ _ _ _ _ _ _ _

2. Write the music symbol for each name below:

_____ Quarter rest	_____ Quarter note
_____ Half note	_____ Half rest
_____ Whole note	_____ Treble clef

WRITE (IMPROVISE) YOUR OWN MUSIC

Practice improvising over the following 8-measure chord sequence (as you did on page 35). The notes for each chord are given in gray at the beginning of each measure to help you find chord tones for your melodies. When you have played the written melody and improvised your own, write your melody in the empty 8 measures. Add words if you like. Use extra staff paper if you need more room.

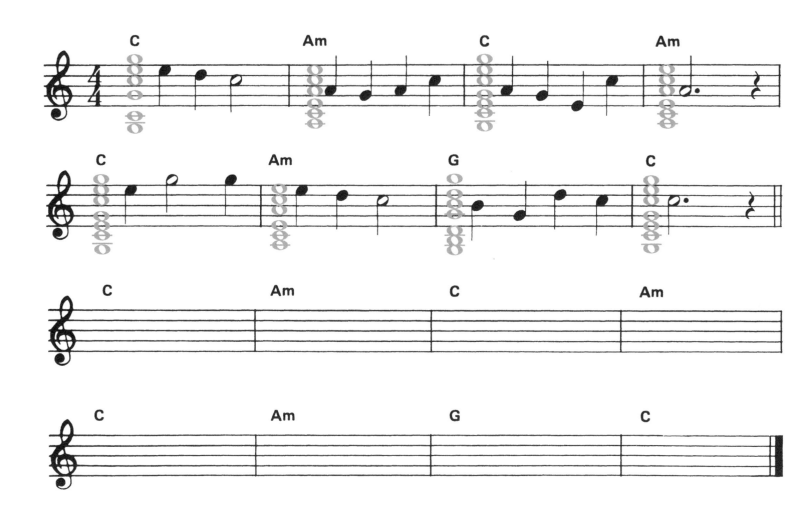

FINGER PICKING

Finger picking is a very popular style of guitar accompaniment which uses **arpeggios** (broken chords) instead of strummed chords. The distinctive sound of finger picking comes from the thumb and fingers plucking only one string each in succession.

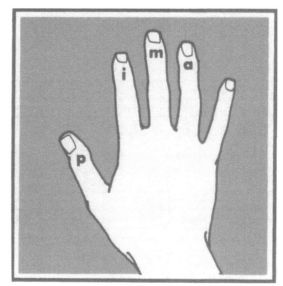

The finger and thumb letters used in this book and in all other Hal Leonard guitar books are based on the internationally accepted system of Spanish words and letters:

p **pulgar** = thumb

i **indice** = index finger

m **medio** = middle finger

a **anular** = ring finger

Follow these steps to learn how to finger pick:

- The thumb (p) plucks strings 4, 5, or 6 depending upon which string is the bass or root of the chord. This motion is a downward stroke. Use the left side of the thumb and thumbnail.
- The other fingers (i, m, a) pluck the string in an upward stroke with the fleshy tip of the finger and fingernail.
- The index finger (i) always plucks string 3.
- The middle finger (m) always plucks string 2.
- The ring finger (a) always plucks string 1.

The thumb and each finger must pluck only one string per stroke and not brush over several strings. (This would be a strum.) Let the strings ring throughout the duration of the chord.

Right-Hand Position

Use a high wrist; arch your palm as if you were holding a ping-pong ball; keep the thumb outside and away from the fingers; and let the fingers do the work rather than lifting your whole hand. See the illustration of page 7.

Keeping in mind the bass string number for each chord (This is the string plucked by the thumb p), practice the pattern below: Work toward an even sound on each string plucked. Each line below represents a guitar string. (The numbers are given at the left.)

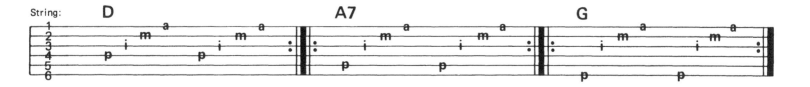

Use the p-i-m-a pattern of finger picking you have just learned as an accompaniment to **The Worried Man Blues.** The pick is indicated under the first line of music to help you see the relationship of one pick per beat to the song above.

The Worried Man Blues

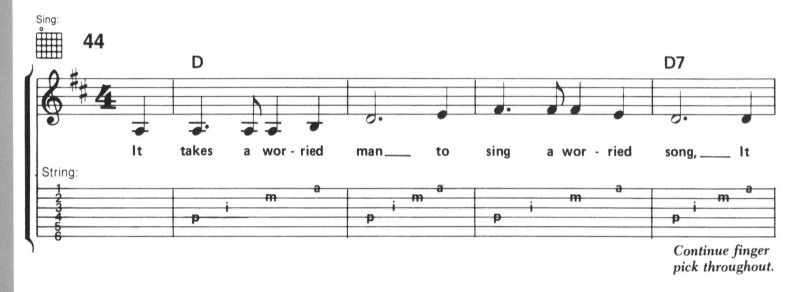

Continue finger pick throughout.

1. **Twenty-nine links of chain around my leg, (3 times)**
   And on each link an initial of my name. *CHORUS*

2. **I asked the judge, "What might be my fine ?" (3 times)**
   "Twenty-one years on the Rocky Mountain Line." *CHORUS*

3. **If anyone should ask you "Who made up this song?"**
   Say, "Twas I, and I sing it all night long." *CHORUS*

When you have thoroughly learned the finger pick written above, try doubling the speed of the right-hand pick so that here are two **p-i-m-a** patterns per measure.

Practice the three-beat finger picking pattern before applying it to **Scarborough Fair**.

Use a simple strum while you are becoming familiar with the chords to **Scarborough Fair**; then, when you are comfortable with both singing and accompanying yourself, apply the finger pick which is written below the first line of music as a sample.

Scarborough Fair

Traditional

Continue finger pick throughout

Am   G   Am   C   Am   D   Am
2. Tell her to make me a cambric shirt,_____   Parsley, sage, rosemary and thyme,
        C   Am   G   Am   D   G   Am
Without any seam or needle work,_____   Then she'll be a true love of mine.

F-Sharp (F#)

HALF AND WHOLE STEPS

The distance between music tones is measured by half-steps and whole-steps. On your guitar the distance between one fret and the next fret is one half-step. The distance from one fret to the second fret in either direction is called a whole-step.

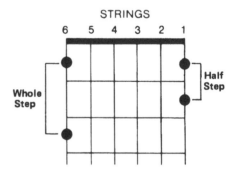

F SHARP (F#)

When a sharp sign (#) is placed in front of a note, the note is raised one half-step. You should play that note up one fret. The note F# on the first space of the staff is played on the fourth string with the fourth finger just behind the fourth fret.

To play F#, think: fourth finger
 fourth string
 fourth fret

also sharp

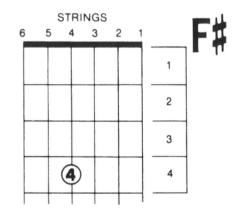

LONDONDERRY AIR

46

Ireland

ANOTHER F SHARP (F#)

The F# on the fifth line of the staff is one octave higher than the F# you just learned. Play this F# by depressing the first string just behind the second fret. Use the tip of your second finger.

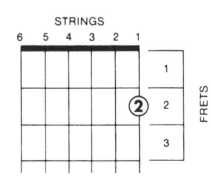

A sharp placed before a note affects all the notes on the same line or space that follow in that measure.

64

Key Signatures

Instead of writing a sharp sign before every F in a song, one sharp is placed at the beginning of the line. This is called a key signature and indicates that every F in the song should be played as F#. In Shenendoah there will be an arrow above each F# to remind you to play F#. Be sure to practice the melody first, then play the melody and chords. Later you can sing and strum the chords.

47

SHENANDOAH

Oh, Shen - an - doah,_____ I long to see you,_____ A - -

way,_____ you roll - ing riv - er,_____ Oh, Shen - an - doah,__

_____ I long to see you,_____ A - way,_____ I'm bound a -

way,_____ 'cross the wide Mis - sou - - ri._____

Remember to play all F's as F# when there is a key signature of one sharp. Practice carefully so there is no hesitation before the chords.

48

GOLDEN GUITAR

I WALK THE LINE

Words and Music by
Johnny Cash

NOWHERE MAN

By John Lennon
and Paul McCartney

THE A CHORD

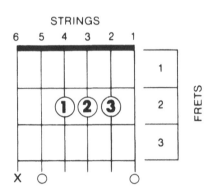

The A major chord is a lot like the A7 chord with the space (string 3) filled in. Arch your fingers so the 1st string rings as an open string. The 5th string is the bass note for the A chord.

The following song, **Yellow Submarine**, uses a variation on the basic down/up strum you already know. The difference lies in the uneven rhythm which is used: (This is the same rhythm as "Mine eyes have seen the glory of the coming of the Lord" from the **Battle Hymn of the Republic.**)

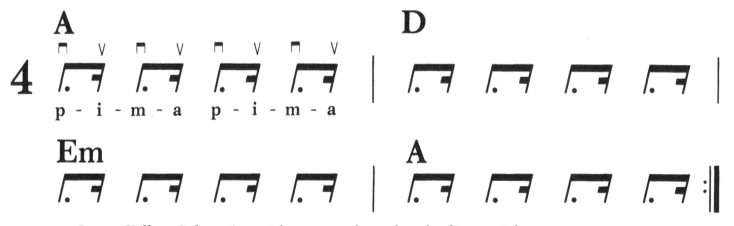

Bump - ty   Bump - ty   Bump - ty   Bump - ty

This same rhythm (sometimes called "dotted" rhythm because it uses dotted notes) can be applied to the finger pick, **p-i-m-a**, used twice in each measure. Practice the following chord sequence first with the down/up strum, then with the finger pick:

Learn **Yellow Submarine** with strums; then play the finger pick.

Yellow Submarine

By John Lennon and Paul McCartney

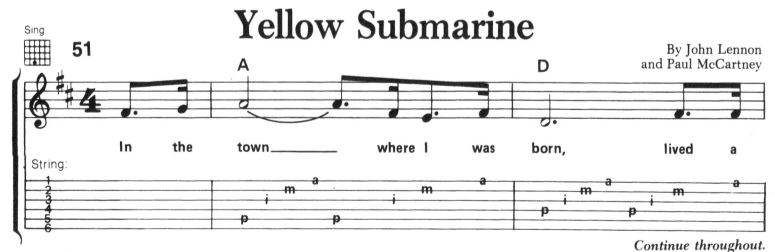

In the town_____ where I was born, lived a

Continue throughout.

Sing and Strum

69

More Guitar Solos

One way to make your playing sound fuller and more advanced is to combine the melody with parts of chords you know. In the following exercises the melody note is on top and the partial chords are added below this note. All of these except the last one are played on open strings 2, 3, and 4. Play the last chord as you would play a full G chord and strum strings 6 through 3.

FAREWELL TO TARWAITHIE

52

Scotland

Be sure to practice the melody and the chords separately; then combine them. Keep the tempo steady even if you need to play slower at first.

Remember that a quarter rest indicates silence for one beat.

THE 3-CORNERED HAT

53

Germany

When you played chords before, you strummed one chord for each beat in the measure. You can vary the strumming by alternating between a bass note (usually the lowest note of a chord and the name of the chord) and the remainder of the chord. Play the C chord example in this way picking the fifth string C and strumming the rest of the chord.

Practice the melody and the chord accompaniment separately; then play them as a duet.

ROW, ROW, ROW YOUR BOAT

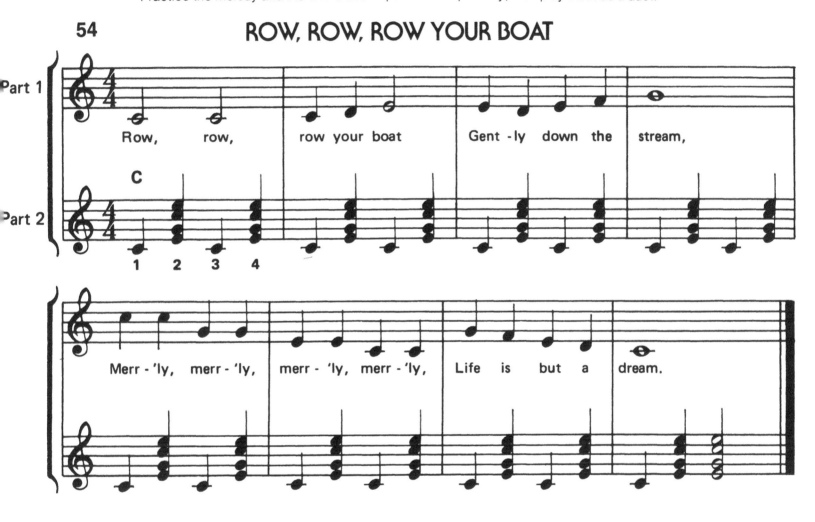

54

Part 1 / Part 2

C

Row, row, row your boat Gent-ly down the stream,

Merr-'ly, merr-'ly, merr-'ly, merr-'ly, Life is but a dream.

The solo below combines parts 1 and 2 above. This type of guitar solo places the melody in the bass. The afterbeats are used to fill in beats when the melody is holding a note. In this exercise the bracket (⎿_____⏌) under the notes is a reminder that is is easier to play if you hold down the full C chord in those sections.

ROW, ROW, ROW YOUR BOAT

55

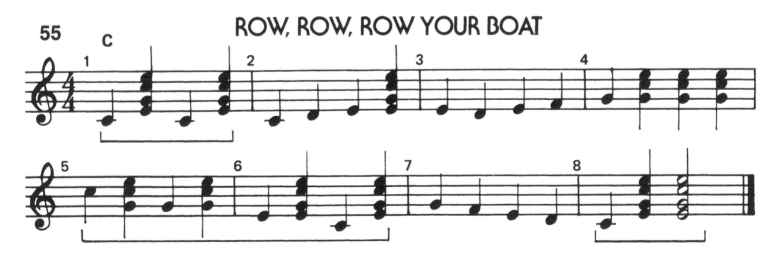

71

THE Dm CHORD

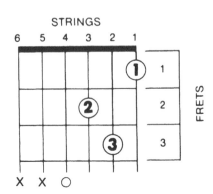

The bass string for the Dm chord is the 4th string. Strum strings 4 through 1.

Use a combination of two different strums on the sea shanty, **The Drunken Sailor:**

Sing:

56

Drunken Sailor

2. **Put him in the brig until he's sober (3) ear-lye in the morning.** *CHORUS*

3. **Put him in the scuppers with the hosepipe on him (3)** *CHORUS*

4. **Shave his belly with a rusty razor (3)** *CHORUS*

Strum: 4

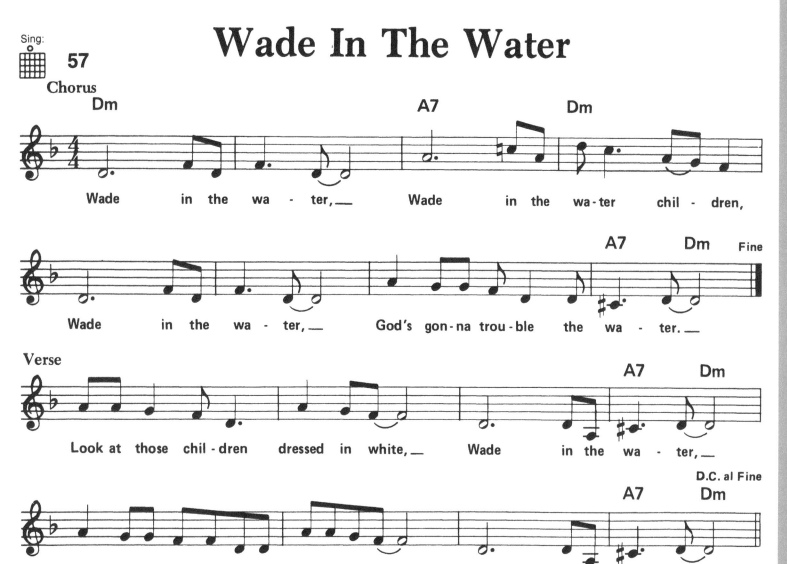

Wade In The Water

Dm
2. Look at those children dressed in black, Wade in the water,
   A7 Dm
   Must be the hippocrites turnin' back, Wade in the water. *CHORUS.*

Dm
3. Look at those children dressed in red, Wade in the water,
   A7 Dm
   Must be the people that Moses led, Wade in the water. *CHORUS.*

4. If I could I surely would, Wade in the water,
   Stand on the rock where Moses stood, Wade in the water. *CHORUS.*

5. The enemy's great, but my Captain's strong, Wade in the water,
   I'm marchin' to the city and the road ain't long, Wade in the water. *CHORUS.*

6. One of these days 'bout twelve o'clock, Wade in the water,
   This old world is gonna reel and rock, Wade in the water. *CHORUS.*

73

THE E CHORD

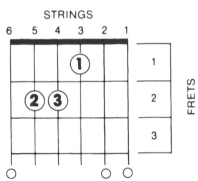

STRINGS
6 5 4 3 2 1
FRETS
1 2 3

The E chord is played with the same finger formation as the Am chord you know, except that the fingers are moved one string over to strings 3, 4, and 5. The bass note is played on the 6th string.

D.S. al Coda is a musical direction sign which tells you to go back to the sign 𝄋 ; then play through the first three lines until you take the 2nd ending; where you see another sign ⊕ which tells you to go to the Coda (the last two lines on page 41). Follow the musical roadmap with your eyes before playing.

Hey Jude

Words and Music by
John Lennon and Paul McCartney

(the last two lines on page 41)

SING AND STRUM

Hey | Jude,_____ don't make it bad, take a sad song_
Jude,_____ don't be a-fraid, you were made to_

Continue throughout

_____ and make it bet-ter._____ Re-mem-ber to
_____ go out and get her._____ The min-ute you

let her in-to your heart, then you can start_____ to
let her un-der your skin, then you be-gin_____ to

make it_____ bet - ter._____ Hey
make it_____ bet - ter._____

To Coda after D.S. ⊕

Eighth Notes

A note that receives ½ beat is called an eighth note. Single eighth notes are written like quarter notes with a flag ♪ ♪ Two or more eighth notes are written with a beam instead of flags.

Since quarter notes receive one beat, there are two eighth notes per beat. An easy way to count eighth notes is 1 & 2 & 3 & 4 &. Tap your foot on the beat. Practice playing quarter notes and eighth notes in the following example.

COUNT: 1 2 3 4   1 & 2 & 3 & 4 &

PRETORIA

59

You have been playing all notes and chords with a downstroke (⊓) of the pick. It is usually easier if you will play eighth notes with one downstroke (⊓) and one upstroke (V).

Play the next exercise with an alternating down and upstroke for all eighth notes and a downstroke for all quarter notes. It may help if you think that your pick is tied to your toe. When you tap your foot on the beat, the pick goes down. When your foot goes up on "and," your pick goes up.

Always practice slowly and steadily at first; then gradually increase the speed.

KOOKABURRA

Australia

Always check the key signature before you begin. All F's should be played F# in BOOGIE
BASS.

BOOGIE BASS

61

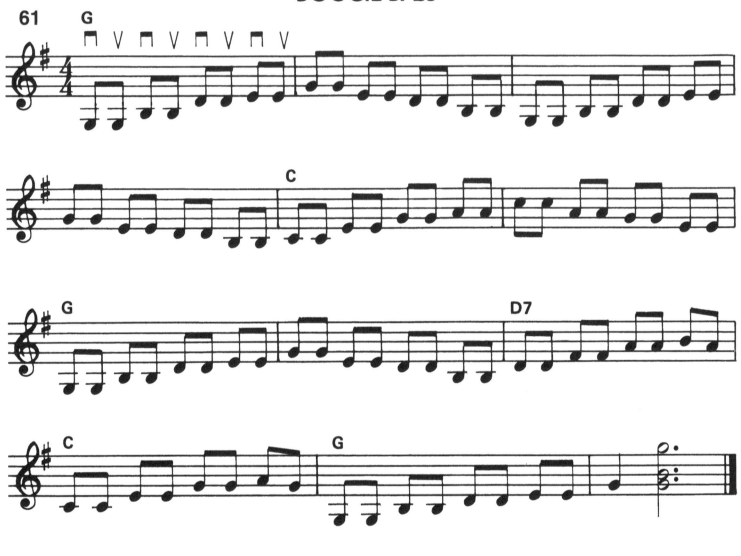

CHANUKAH SONG

Jewish

62

Did you play F#'s?

Guitar Ensemble

3-PART ROUND

63

Add a fourth part by playing this pattern throughout:

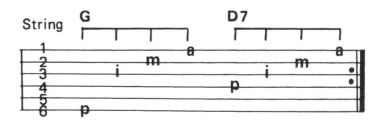

3-PART ROUND

64

Add a fourth part by playing this finger picking pattern:

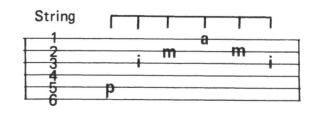

HEARTBREAKER

Words and Music by
Carole Bayer Sager and David Wolfert

FEELINGS
(¿ DIME?)

English Words and Music by Morris Albert
Spanish Lyric by Thomas Fundora

The Rainbow Connection

By Paul Williams
and Kenny Ascher

Sing:

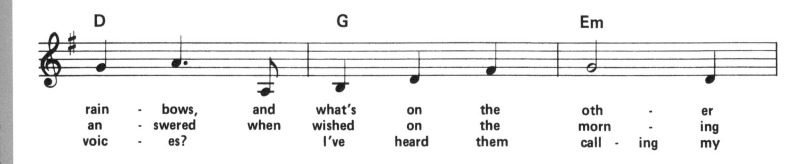

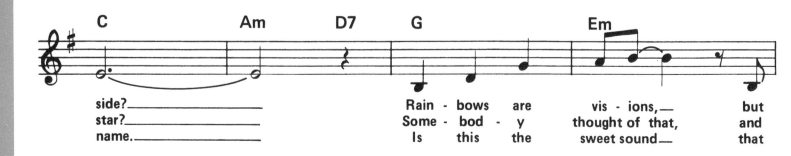

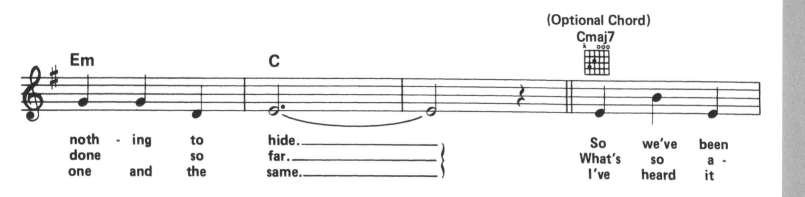

noth - ing to hide._____ So we've been
done so far._____ What's so a -
one and the same._____ I've heard it

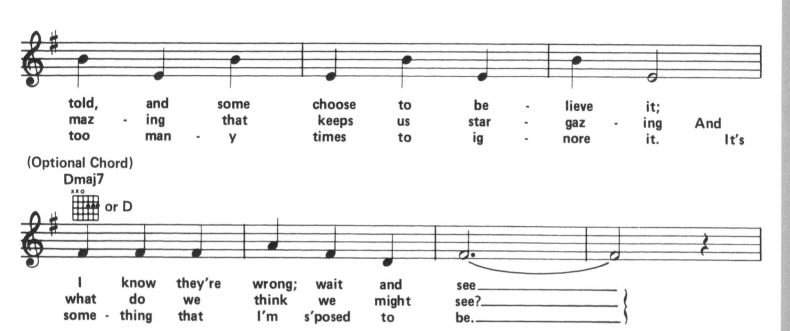

told, and some choose to be - lieve it;
maz - ing some that keeps us star - gaz - ing And
too man - y times to ig - nore it. It's

I know they're wrong; wait and see_____
what do we think we might see?_____
some - thing that I'm s'posed to be._____

Some - day we'll find it, the rain - bow con -

nec - tion; The lov - ers, the dream - ers,____ and

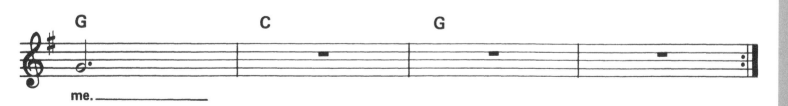

me._____

83

SHADOWS IN THE MOONLIGHT

Words and Music by
Charlie Black and Rory Bourke

We'll be shad-ows in the moon- light, dar-ling, I'll meet you at____ mid- night,_____ hand in hand we'll go danc- in' through the milk- y way._____ And we'll find a lit- tle hide- a- way where we can love the whole____ night a- way._____ We'll be shad-ows in the moon- light right up 'til the light of day._____ Ooo, the night is young and ba- by so are we, glad, I'm gon- na make you glad you came. We'll be

"So Long, It's Been Good To Know You" is a famous dust bowl ballad of the 1930's. This arrangement of the chorus is written an octave higher than usual so that you can play the melody easily. When you sing and play the chords as accompaniment, sing the melody an octave lower than written.

When you have mastered the melody and can easily strum the chords, try playing a bass note-afterbeat chord accompaniment in $\frac{3}{4}$ time. Play the bass note on beat one and afterbeat strums on beats two and three. First practice each chord/measure below separately; then combine them as an exercise.

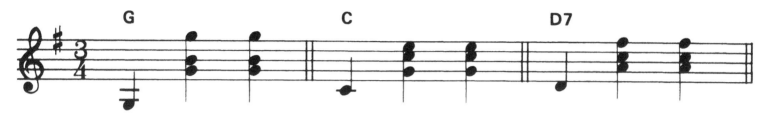

Now try this accompaniment to "So Long."

SO LONG
It's Been Good To Know Yuh

69

Sing an octave lower.

Words and Music by
Woody Guthrie

So _____ long _____ it's been good to know you, _____

So _____ long _____ it's been good to know you. _____

So _____ long _____ it's been good to know you, what a

long, _____ long time _____ since I've _____ been home, _____ And I

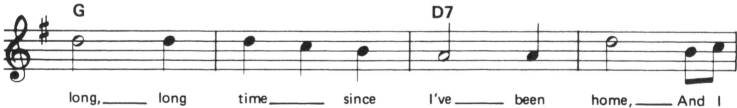

got to be drift - ing a - long. _____

THE B7 CHORD

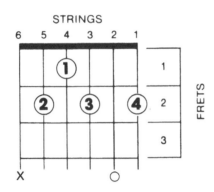

STRINGS
6 5 4 3 2 1

B7 is your first four-finger chord. Notice that the 2nd-fret fingers are placed on strings 1, 3 and 5. Keeping this visual pattern in mind will help you move to this chord quickly. When you change from E to B7, keep the 2nd finger down. The bass string for B7 is the 5th string.

Ramblin' Round

Words by Woody Guthrie
Music based on "Goodnight Irene" by
Huddie Ledbetter and John A. Lomax

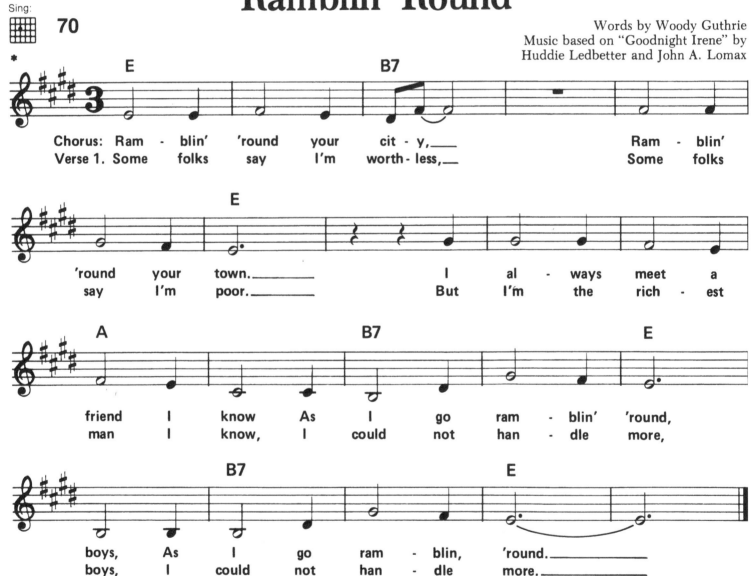

Sing:
70

Chorus: Ram - blin' 'round your cit - y,___ Ram - blin'
Verse 1. Some folks say I'm worth-less,___ Some folks

'round your town._____ I al - ways meet a
say I'm poor._____ But I'm the rich - est

friend I know As I go ram - blin' 'round,
man I know, I could not han - dle more,

boys, As I go ram - blin, 'round._____
boys, I could not han - dle more._____

*Use the bass note/after strum (3 ♩ / /) accompaniment.

2. Some folks long for silver, Some folks long for gold.
   But all I want's a life that's free,
   And I will never grow old, boys, And I will never grow old.

3. (Why not try making up a verse or two of your own?)

SING AND STRUM

THE E7 CHORD

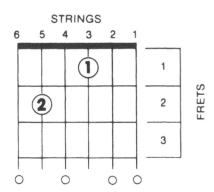

There are two ways of playing the E7 chord — either as a subtraction from or an addition to the E chord you already know. The four-finger version is preferable if you are finger picking. The bass note for E7 is the 6th string.

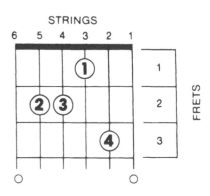

The **12-bar blues** form (12 measures) is one of the most important forms of American music. Notice the three phrases of four measures each and that the first line of text repeats followed by a rhyming line (AAB). After you have thoroughly absorbed the chord progression and the feel of the song, try making up some of your own verses. 12-bar blues became the basis for many early rock 'n' roll hits.

Good Mornin' Blues

2. Lay down last night, tryin' to take my rest, (2 times)
   My mind kept ramblin' like the wild geese in the west.

3. The sun gonna shine on my back door some day. (2 times)
   The wind gonna rise up and blow my blues away.

*Use a down/up strum with a dotted rhythm (4 ♪♪ ♪♪ ♪♪ ♪♪).

87

THE MASTERPIECE

(The T.V. Theme from THE MASTERPIECE THEATER)

By J.J. Mouret
and Paul Parnes

*Options: Play part 1 as a solo. Add a third player on the chords.
Tape record one part, and play a duet with yourself.

Two New Notes... C♯ and D♯

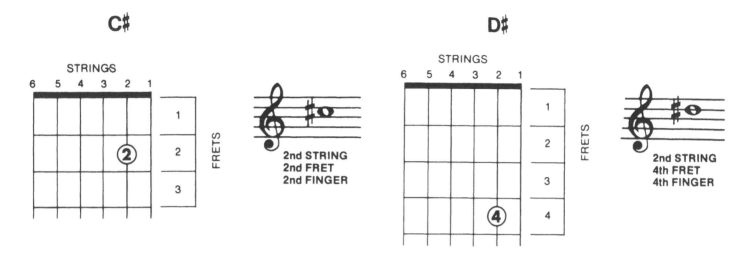

C♯

STRINGS
6 5 4 3 2 1

FRETS
1
② 2
3

2nd STRING
2nd FRET
2nd FINGER

D♯

STRINGS
6 5 4 3 2 1

FRETS
1
2
3
④ 4

2nd STRING
4th FRET
4th FINGER

In many songs there will be notes in a few measures that should be played as sharps, but are not a part of the key signature. These added sharps are called **accidentals**. In this song, the C♯ and D♯ in measure 2 are accidentals. Remember to play F♯ all the way through.

73

YESTERDAY

Words and Music by
John Lennon and Paul McCartney

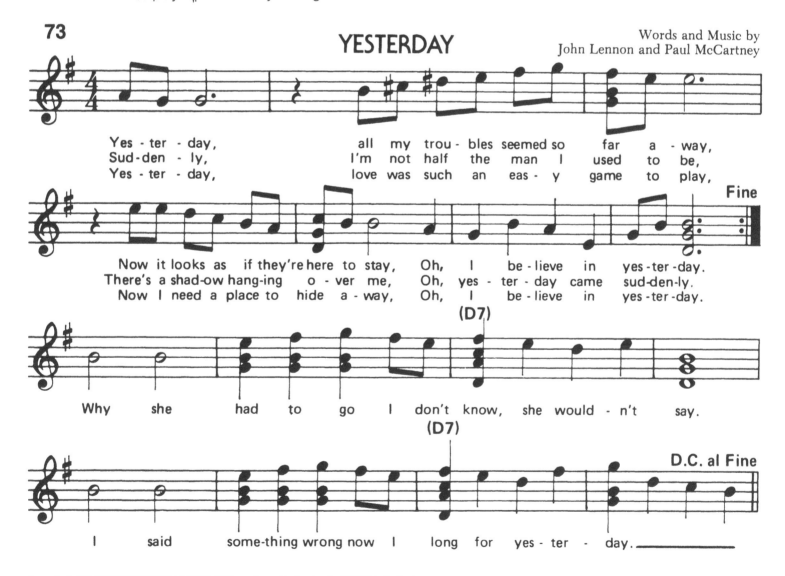

Yes - ter - day,   all my trou - bles seemed so   far   a - way,
Sud - den - ly,   I'm not half the man I   used to be,
Yes - ter - day,   love was such an eas - y   game to play,

Fine

Now it looks as if they're here to stay, Oh, I   be - lieve in   yes - ter - day.
There's a shad-ow hang-ing o - ver me, Oh, yes - ter - day came sud-den-ly.
Now I need a place to hide a - way, Oh, I   be - lieve in   yes - ter - day.

(D7)

Why   she   had   to   go   I don't know, she would - n't   say.

(D7)

D.C. al Fine

I   said   some-thing wrong now I   long for yes - ter - day.____

COUNTRY BOY
(You Got Your Feet In L.A.)

Words and Music by
Dennis Lambert and Brian Potter

THE F CHORD

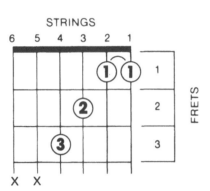

STRINGS

Unlike other chords you have played, the F chord has two strings depressed by one finger. The first finger forms a small "bar" across strings 1 and 2. You will find that it is easier to roll this finger slightly so that the strings are depressed by the outside rather than the flat underside of the 1st finger. The bass note for F is the 4th string.

You Needed Me

Words and Music by
Randy Goodrum

Sing:
75
Option: Capo 2 or 3

Continue throughout

I cried a tear, you wiped it dry.
hand when it was cold.

I was con - fused you cleared my mind.
When I was lost you took me home.

I sold my soul you bought it back for me
You gave me hope when I was at the end,

and held me up and gave me dig - ni - ty.
and turned my lies back in - to truth a - gain.

Some - how you need - ed me.
You ev - en called me friend.

You gave me strength

93

MUSIC SYMBOLS AND TERMS

Bar Line	The vertical line that separates measures.
Chord	Simultaneous sounding of 3 or more notes.
Coda ⊕	The ending section of a piece of music.
D.C. al Fine	**Da Capo** (to the beginning) **al Fine** (until the end). Return to the beginning and play to the **Fine.**
D.S. al Fine	**Dal Segno** (to the sign 𝄋 ; then play to the **Fine.**
Down Stroke ⊓	
Fine	The end.
Half Step	The smallest interval on the guitar — the distance from one fret to the next.
Harmony	the system of chords that underlies the melody.
Key Signature	The placement of sharps or flats at the beginning of each staff.
Ledger Lines	The lines used above or below the staff to extend the range of notes.
Measure (also known as Bar)	The distance from one bar line to the next.
Melody	A string of pitches or notes.
Notes	Whole: 𝅝 Half: 𝅗𝅥 Quarter: 𝅘𝅥 Eighth: 𝅘𝅥𝅮 or 𝅘𝅥𝅮𝅘𝅥𝅮
Open String	A string which is not depressed by a finger.
Pickup Notes	Any notes which form an incomplete measure at the beginning of a song.
Pitch	The highness or lowness of sound which is determined by the number of vibrations per second.
Rests	Whole: ▬ Half: ▬ Quarter: 𝄽 Eighth: 𝄾
Sharp ♯	Raises the pitch one-half step.
Staff ≣	Five lines and four spaces.
Syncopation	Off-beat accents
Tempo	The speed or pace of the music
Tie 𝅗𝅥‿𝅘𝅥	A curved line that connects two notes of the same pitch.
Time signature (meter signature) 4/4 3/4	A stack of two numbers that tells what kind of note gets a beat and how many beats there are in one measure.
Transposition	Changing the key (tonal center) of a piece. Raising or lowering the whole piece.
Treble clef 𝄞	Locates the note G on the second line of the staff.
Up Stroke ∨	
Whole step	The interval between one note and another two frets higher or lower. The equivalent of two half-steps.

Chord Chart

In this chart you will find all of the chords you learned in this book. There are also several of the more common chords you may see in other music you are playing.

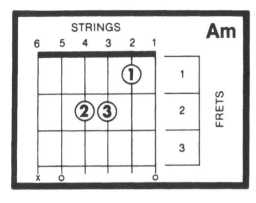

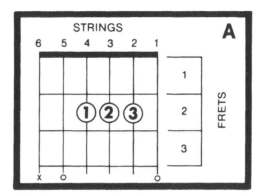

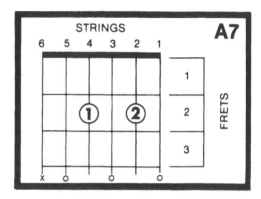

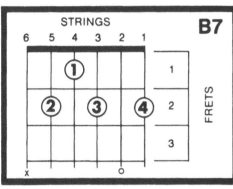

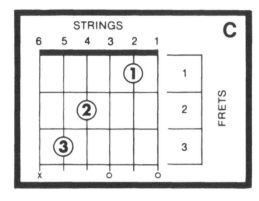

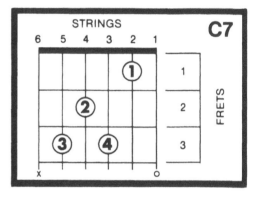

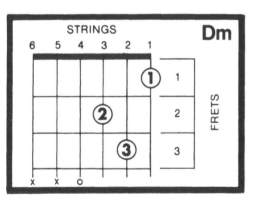

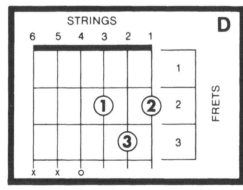

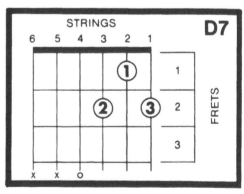

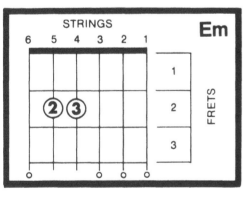

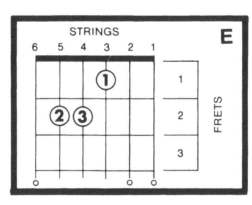

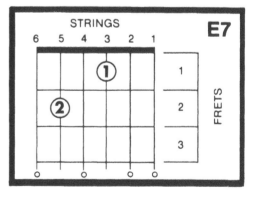

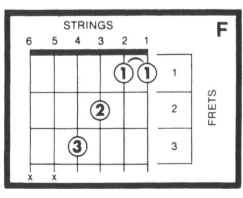

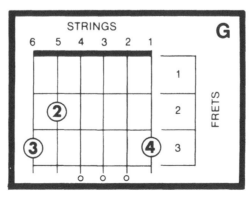

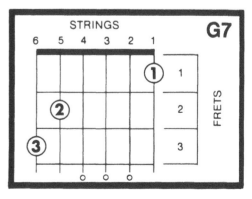

HAL LEONARD GUITAR METHOD

METHOD BOOKS, SONGBOOKS AND REFERENCE BOOKS

THE HAL LEONARD GUITAR METHOD is designed for anyone just learning to play acoustic or electric guitar. It is based on years of teaching guitar students of all ages, and it also reflects some of the best guitar teaching ideas from around the world. This comprehensive method includes: A learning sequence carefully paced with clear instructions; popular songs which increase the incentive to learn to play; versatility – can be used as self-instruction or with a teacher; audio accompaniments so that students have fun and sound great while practicing.

BOOK 1
00699010	Book Only	$9.99
00699027	Book/Online Audio	$14.99
00697341	Book/Online Audio + DVD	$27.99
00697318	DVD Only	$19.99
00155480	Deluxe Beginner Edition (Book, CD, DVD, Online Audio/ Video & Chord Poster)	$22.99

COMPLETE (BOOKS 1, 2 & 3)
00699040	Book Only	$19.99
00697342	Book/Online Audio	$27.99

BOOK 2
00699020	Book Only	$9.99
00697313	Book/Online Audio	$14.99

BOOK 3
00699030	Book Only	$9.99
00697316	Book/Online Audio	$14.99

Prices, contents and availability subject to change without notice.

STYLISTIC METHODS

ACOUSTIC GUITAR
00697347 Method Book/Online Audio $19.99
00237969 Songbook/Online Audio $17.99

BLUEGRASS GUITAR
00697405 Method Book/Online Audio $19.99

BLUES GUITAR
00697326 Method Book/Online Audio (9" x 12") . $16.99
00697344 Method Book/Online Audio (6" x 9")... $15.99
00697385 Songbook/Online Audio (9" x 12")...... $16.99
00248636 Kids Method Book/Online Audio $14.99

BRAZILIAN GUITAR
00697415 Method Book/Online Audio $17.99

CHRISTIAN GUITAR
00695947 Method Book/Online Audio $17.99

CLASSICAL GUITAR
00697376 Method Book/Online Audio $16.99

COUNTRY GUITAR
00697337 Method Book/Online Audio $24.99

FINGERSTYLE GUITAR
00697378 Method Book/Online Audio $22.99
00697432 Songbook/Online Audio $19.99

FLAMENCO GUITAR
00697363 Method Book/Online Audio $17.99

FOLK GUITAR
00697414 Method Book/Online Audio $16.99

JAZZ GUITAR
00695359 Book/Online Audio $22.99
00697386 Songbook/Online Audio $16.99

JAZZ-ROCK FUSION
00697387 Book/Online Audio $24.99

R&B GUITAR
00697356 Book/Online Audio $19.99
00697433 Songbook/CD Pack $16.99

ROCK GUITAR
00697319 Book/Online Audio $19.99
00697383 Songbook/Online Audio $19.99

ROCKABILLY GUITAR
00697407 Book/Online Audio $19.99

OTHER METHOD BOOKS

BARITONE GUITAR METHOD
00242055 Book/Online Audio $12.99

GUITAR FOR KIDS
00865003 Method Book 1/Online Audio $14.99
00697402 Songbook/Online Audio $12.99
00128437 Method Book 2/Online Audio $14.99

MUSIC THEORY FOR GUITARISTS
00695790 Book/Online Audio $22.99

TENOR GUITAR METHOD
00148330 Book/Online Audio $14.99

12-STRING GUITAR METHOD
00249528 Book/Online Audio $22.99

METHOD SUPPLEMENTS

ARPEGGIO FINDER
00697352 6" x 9" Edition $9.99
00697351 9" x 12" Edition $10.99

BARRE CHORDS
00697406 Book/Online Audio $16.99

CHORD, SCALE & ARPEGGIO FINDER
00697410 Book Only $24.99

GUITAR TECHNIQUES
00697389 Book/Online Audio $16.99

INCREDIBLE CHORD FINDER
00697200 6" x 9" Edition $7.99
00697208 9" x 12" Edition $9.99

INCREDIBLE SCALE FINDER
00695568 6" x 9" Edition $9.99
00695490 9" x 12" Edition $9.99

LEAD LICKS
00697345 Book/Online Audio $12.99

RHYTHM RIFFS
00697346 Book/Online Audio $14.99

SONGBOOKS

CLASSICAL GUITAR PIECES
00697388 Book/Online Audio $12.99

EASY POP MELODIES
00697281 Book Only $7.99
00697440 Book/Online Audio $16.99

(MORE) EASY POP MELODIES
00697280 Book Only $7.99
00697269 Book/Online Audio $16.99

(EVEN MORE) EASY POP MELODIES
00699154 Book Only $7.99
00697439 Book/Online Audio $16.99

EASY POP RHYTHMS
00697336 Book Only $10.99
00697441 Book/Online Audio $16.99

(MORE) EASY POP RHYTHMS
00697338 Book Only $9.99
00697322 Book/Online Audio $16.99

(EVEN MORE) EASY POP RHYTHMS
00697340 Book Only $9.99
00697323 Book/Online Audio $16.99

EASY POP CHRISTMAS MELODIES
00697417 Book Only $12.99
00697416 Book/Online Audio $16.99

EASY POP CHRISTMAS RHYTHMS
00278177 Book Only $6.99
00278175 Book/Online Audio $14.99

EASY SOLO GUITAR PIECES
00110407 Book Only $12.99

REFERENCE

GUITAR PRACTICE PLANNER
00697401 Book Only $7.99

GUITAR SETUP & MAINTENANCE
00697427 6" x 9" Edition $16.99
00697421 9" x 12" Edition $14.99

For more info, songlists, or to purchase these and more books from your favorite music retailer, go to

halleonard.com

HAL•LEONARD®